First of all,
gratulate you tor purchasing this unique
book: I Want To: Know Like God, Speak
Like God and Do Like God.

This inspirational, creative and unique
work will be a blessing to any family member
or friend. I know you will enjoy each
and every word. It's a great gift for any occasion!

This book is printed by request and is not
sold in stores. If you would like to purchase
a copy of this book or additional
copies, you may do so by filling out the order
form in the back of this book.

Due to great demands, please allow two to
three weeks for your order to be filled.

Remember! Put Your Order In Today!

Barbara L. Jefferson

Cover design and book production by
Jefferson Outreach Ministries & Publications
Jesus Operates Miracles Profoundly/JOMP

Barbara J's Books of Deliverance
I Want To: Know Like God,
Speak Like God & Do Like God

Jefferson Outreach Ministries
& Publications
Chicago, Illinois 60628
E-mail:jomplb@sbcglobal.net

ISBN-13
978-0-9818309-0-2
ISBN-10
0-9818309-0-0

Printed in the United States of America

Barbara J's

Books

Of

Deliverance

He that dwelleth in the secret place of the most High

Jefferson Outreach Ministries & Publications

LJ

BJ

Covenant

O M

Jesus Operate Miracles Profoundly

Shall abide under the shadow of the Almighty

Minister Barbara L. Jefferson

<u>My Mandate</u>

But rise and stand upon thy feet: For I have appeared unto thee for this purpose, to make thee a minister and a witness both of these things which thou hast seen, and of those things in which I will appear unto thee.

Delivering thee from the people, and from the Gentiles, unto whom now I send thee, to open their eyes, and to turn them from darkness to light, and from the power of Satan unto God, that they may receive forgiveness of sins, and inheritance among them which are sanctified by faith that is in me.

Acts 26:16-18
Jesus Operates Miracles Profoundly

Comments From
<u>The Author</u>

I was inspired by the Lord to write this book for those of you who want to see yourselves go to another level. This book is written to build your faith, strengthen, edify and encourage you.

This book will show you where you are in your walk with the Lord. Most of all, this book is for you to become that man or woman that Father God has called you to be.

This book was written by the inspiration of the Holy Ghost. It is to comfort, exalt, build your confidence, and to bring you to a new level in God. If you want victory, open your heart, mind and ears to hear what the Holy Spirit is saying.

Acknowledgment

You must understand that the only way to fulfill your destiny is to First of all, know what your calling is and to wait on it. Begin to visualize yourself in that which God has called you to do.

My mistake was disregarding the visions God would continually show me. Praying for people who were in despair and laying hands on the sick.

I did not want to be in-self or in my flesh, but I wanted to please God. Who was I to speak into someone's life for deliverance? It took prayer, fasting and finally submitting to the calling God has on my life.

Secondly, learn how to develop your spirit to hear God's instructions. How do you know you are hearing yourself or the Lord?

It is all in his word!

My desire was to know how to meditate in the word, but I just could not understand meditating in the scriptures.

As a young woman, I took up meditation and relaxation techniques years before I gave my life to the Lord.

I realized that sitting quietly and reciting or uttering aloud God's word in place of metaphysical or relaxation techniques was my answer. This was meditating in the scriptures!

That is when I received <u>MY</u> breakthrough, it was like a light bulb went off in my head, and my eyes were finally opened.

You can read books by every teacher, pastor and tele-evangelist, but for some of us it will have to be a personal experience that will finally set you free.

I also exercise Romans 10:8 - But what saith it? The word is nigh thee, even in thy

mouth, and in thy heart: that is, the word of faith, which we preach.

My pastor, Apostle Richard D. Henton began to teach us about the recipe; to confess with thy mouth, and believe in thine heart. For with the heart man believeth unto righteousness: and with the mouth confession is made unto salvation. Romans 10:9-10.

After Learning this I began to see the manifestations of the scriptures bringing my gifts forward, and excitement automatically took over. It is also your responsibility to exercise your gift, and to be a good steward over it.

You will be ready and willing to operate in that gift which God has chosen for you. Whether it be a deliverance ministry or a ministry of helps, the word of God will be there for you to succeed.

These are just some of the scriptures that I have used in my ministry, and I wanted to share them with you.

I hope these scriptures will enhance your personal relationship with God, and that you may be able to receive his instructions for your life.

I am a telephone counselor at my church, and I pray for those who are in despair, who need healing and deliverance. I also speak into their lives God's Word!

I find that when I personalize the scriptures they always renew my mind faster, and I also visualize myself in my calling.

When I need encouragement or edification the scripture that I lean on is:

Psalm 91:1

He that dwelleth in the secret place of the most High shall abide under the shadow of the Almighty.

The Condition

You must understand that there is a condition that you have to respect. When God says **If You** that is a condition.

You must full fill the **If You** first before you can receive the promise or the fruit of the word.

Deuteronomy 28:1

And it shall come to pass, **If** thou shalt harken diligently unto the voice of the Lord thy God, to observe and to do all his commandments, which I command thee this day, that the Lord thy God will set thee on high above all nations of the earth.

This condition is not only for you to receive a blessing, but to position you to also be a blessing to the people of God.

Joshua 1:8

This book of the law shall not depart out of thy mouth; but thou shalt meditate therein day and night, that thou mayest observe to do according to all that is written therein: for then thou shalt make thy way prosperous, and then thou shalt have good success.

The Lord informs you that if you follow these instructions not only will you be prosperous, but you will also have good success which will come though wisdom.

Matthew 18:19

Again I say unto you, that **If** two of you shall agree on earth as touching any thing that they shall ask, it shall be done for them of my Father which is in heaven.

Here the Lord states that you and one other only need to touch and agree for a thing and it shall be done.

St. John 15:7

If ye abide in me, and my words abide in you, ye shall ask what ye will, and it shall be done unto you.

This **If** is for only you. You must spend time with the word of God, in prayer, and worship. A personal relationship is what He is looking for, and you will know the desire that God has for you.

Romans: 10-9

That **If** thou shalt confess with thy mouth the Lord Jesus, and shalt believe in thine heart that God hath raised him from the dead, thou shalt be saved.

In order to receive salvation you must acknowledge that Jesus is the Son of God, and that God has raised him from the grave.

These were just a few examples of the **If**

you condition. There are several more

that you can look up on your own.

You may only want to concentrate on one section of the book at a time. I believe certain scriptures should be meditated on everyday, so you will see many of the same verses repeated in each section.

When we teach others to pray, we always tell them to speak God's word back to him, because His word does not return unto him void. There may be someone who does not know how to confess the word back to God, so I have confessed it for you.

I have only used these scriptures, but you can make your own confessions that is especially made for your situation. Some scriptures are all ready personalized, and will not have a personal confession.

If you apply these meditation scriptures to your daily life, I believe you will see a difference in the way you live.

I WANT TO:
KNOW LIKE GOD,
SPEAK LIKE GOD
& DO LIKE GOD

Dedication

I would like to dedicate this book to my husband, Larry, who foresaw this work. I also want to thank mother, Ethel E. Henton, who along with my husband encouraged me and gave me counsel, without their help it could not have been.

Thank you, I love you both!

I thank my Father God for
this creation

The Son of God for his anointing

The Holy Ghost for his inspiration

I WANT TO: KNOW LIKE GOD,
SPEAK LIKE GOD & DO LIKE GOD

Contents

I WANT TO:

TO

KNOW

LIKE

GOD

Have you ever held a conversation with someone, and afterwards they said "You must have been talking to the Lord about me. You answered my question that I asked the Lord about what I should do in this situation."

Or have you ever had someone ask you "How did you know what happened to me, and in such detail?"

Did you know why someone would mistreat, or lied on you, and you found out it was the spirit of jealously.

There were times when I was out shopping, or at the doctor's, and a conversation would begin, and before you knew it I would be ministering to someone. Answering a question or speaking into their life. In the beginning I didn't know I was answering their questions, or speaking into their life.

All of these thing happen to me on a regular basis. I had to learn how to recognize each one.

1Corinthians 12:3-12

Wherefore I give you to understand, that no man speaking by the Spirit of God calleth Jesus accursed: and that no man can say that Jesus is the Lord, but by the Holy Ghost.

Now there are diversities of gifts, but the same Spirit.

And there are differences of administrations, but the same Lord.

And there are diversities of operations, but it is the same God which worketh all in all.

But the manifestation of the Spirit is given to every man to profit withal.

For to one is given by the Spirit the word of wisdom; to another the word of knowledge by the same Spirit;

To another faith by the same Spirit; to another the gifts of healing by the same Spirit;

To another the working of miracles; to another prophecy; to another discerning of spirits; to another divers kinds of tongues; to another the interpretation of tongues:

But all these worketh that one and the selfsame Spirit, dividing to every man severally as he will.

For as the body is one, and hath many members, and all the members of that one body, being many are one body; so also is Christ.

The Word of Wisdom

God supernaturally reveals His future purpose though a man or a woman in Christ that can't conceptualize the divine purposes of God in Christ on their own.

(Daniel 2:19-20) (Daniel 28:30)
(Daniel 5:17-31)

The Word of Knowledge

God supernaturally reveals though a man or woman in Christ a present or past fact that they would not naturally know on their own.

(Daniel 2:21-22) (Daniel 10:1)

Discerning of Spirits

God supernaturally give insight into the spirit world to reveal what kind of spirit motivates a person, whether their actions are right or wrong.

(1 Corinthians 2:4) (Malachi 3:18)
(Hebrews 4:12)

It is not used for fault finding.

Deuteronomy 28:1

And it shall come to pass, if thou shalt hearken diligently unto the voice of the Lord thy God, to observe and to do all his commandments which I command thee this day, that the Lord thy God will set thee on high above all nations of the earth.

(personal confession)

I confess with my mouth, and believe in my heart that it has come to pass that because I do listen diligently to the voice of the Lord my God, to observe and to do all his commandments which He command me this day, that the Lord my God have set me on high above all nations of the earth: and all these blessings have come upon me, and have overtaken me, I am listening to the voice of the Lord my God.

Joshua 1:5

There shall not any man be able to stand before thee all the days of thy life; as I was with Moses, so I will be with thee: I will not fail thee nor forsake thee.

(personal confession)

I confess with my mouth, and believe in my heart that there shall not any man be able to stand before me all the days of my life; as God was with Moses, so He will be with me: He will not fail me, nor forsake me.

Joshua 1:8

This book of the law shall not depart out of thy mouth; but thou shalt meditate therein day and night, that thou mayest observe to do according to all that is written therein: For then thou shalt make thy way prosperous and then thou shalt have good success.

(personal confession)

I confess with my mouth, and believe in my heart that this book of the law has not departed out of my mouth; but I do meditate day and night, that I mayest observe to do according to all that is written: For now the Lord have made my way prosperous and I do have good success.

II Chronicles 15:7

Be ye strong therefore, and let not your hands be weak: for your work shall be rewarded.

(personal confession)

I confess with my mouth, and believe in my heart that I am strong, and I let not my hands become weak: for my work is rewarded.

II Chronicles 16:9

For the eyes of the Lord run to and fro throughout the whole earth, to shew him self strong in the behalf of them whose heart is perfect toward him.

(personal confession)

I confess with my mouth, and believe in my heart that the eyes of the Lord run to and fro throughout the whole earth, to show himself strong in the behalf of me whose heart is perfect toward him.

Job 22:21

Acquaint now thyself with him, and be at peace: thereby good shall come unto thee.

23

(personal confession)

I confess with my mouth, and believe in my heart that I have acquainted myself with God, and I am at peace: thereby good has come to me.

Job 33:14-17

For God speaketh once, yea twice, yet man perceiveth it not. In a dream, in a vision of the night, when deep sleep falleth upon men, in slumberings upon the bed; then he openeth the ears of men, and sealeth their instruction. That he may withdraw man from his purpose, and hide pride from man.

(personal confession)

I confess with my mouth, and believe in my heart that God speaks once, yes twice, yet I perceive it not. In a dream, in a vision of the night, when deep sleep falls upon me, in slumberings upon my bed; Then he opens my ears, and seals my instruction. That he may withdraw me from my purpose, and hide pride from me.

Psalm 19:14

Let the words of my mouth, and the meditation of my heart, be acceptable in thy sight, O Lord, my strength, and my redeemer.

(personal confession)

I confess with my mouth, and believe in my heart that the words of my mouth, and the meditation of my heart, shall be acceptable in thy sight, O Lord, you are my strength, and my redeemer.

Psalm 20:6

Now know I that the Lord saveth his anointed; he will hear him from his holy heaven with the saving strength of his right hand.

(personal confession)

I confess with my mouth, and believe in my heart that now I know that the Lord saveth his anointed; he does hear me from his holy heaven with the saving strength of his right hand.

Psalm 21:2

Thou hast given him his heart's desire, and has not withholden the request of his lips.
(personal confession)

I confess with my mouth, and believe in my heart that the Lord have given me my heart's desire, and has not withheld the request of my lip.

Psalm 25:9

The meek will he guide in judgment: and the meek will he teach his way.
(personal confession)

I confess with my mouth, and believe in my heart that God will guide me in judgment: and He will he teach me his way.

Psalm 25:14

The secret of the Lord is with them that fear him; and he will shew them his covenant.
(personal confession)

I confess with my mouth, and believe in my heart that the secret of the Lord is with me, and he will show me his covenant.

Psalms 32:8

I will instructs thee and teaches thee in the way which thou shalt go: I will guide thee with mine eye.

(personal confession)

I confess with my mouth, and believe in my heart that the Holy Spirit instructs me and teaches me in the way which I shall go: He does guide me with His eye.

Psalm 34-15

The eyes of the Lord are upon the righteous, and his ears are open unto their cry.

(personal confession)

I confess with my mouth, and believe in my heart that the eyes of the Lord are upon the righteous, and his ears are open unto my cry.

Psalm 57:2

I will cry unto God most high; unto God that performeth all things for me.

Psalm 119:18

Open thou mine eyes, that I may behold wondrous things out of thy law.

Psalm 119:105

Thy word is a lamp unto my feet, and a light Unto my path.

Proverbs 2:7

He layeth up sound wisdom for the righteous. He is a buckler to them that walk uprightly.

(personal confession)

I confess with my mouth, and believe in my heart that because I am the righteousness of God that he lays up sound wisdom for me. He is my buckler because I walk uprightly.

Proverbs 3:5

Trust in the Lord with all thine heart; and lean not unto thine own understanding. In all thy ways acknowledge him, and he shall direct thy paths.

(personal confession)

I confess with my mouth, and believe in my heart that I trust in the Lord with all my heart; and I lean not unto my own understanding, but in all my ways I do acknowledge him, and he does direct my paths.

Proverbs 3:13

Happy is the man that findeth wisdom, and the man that getteth understanding.
(personal confession)

I confess with my mouth, and believe in my heart that when I find wisdom and understanding I am happy.

Proverbs 30:5

Every word of God is pure: he is a shield unto them that put their trust in him.
(personal confession)

I confess with my mouth, and believe in my heart that every word of God is pure: he is a shield unto me, I put my trust in him.

Isaiah 11:2

And the spirit of the Lord does rest upon him, the spirit of wisdom and understanding, the spirit of counsel and might, the spirit of knowledge and of the fear of the Lord.

(personal confession)

I confess with my mouth, and believe in my heart that the spirit of the Lord does rest upon me, the spirit of wisdom and understanding, the spirit of counsel and might, the spirit of knowledge and of the fear of the Lord.

Isaiah 48:10

Behold, I have refined thee, but not with silver, I have chosen thee in the furnace of affliction.

(personal confession)

I confess with my mouth, and believe in my heart that the Lord have refined me through my trials and tribulations.

Isaiah 60:1

Arise, shine; for thy light is come, and the glory of the Lord is risen upon thee.

(personal confession)

I confess with my mouth, and believe in my heart that I shall arise and shine,; for my light is come, and the glory of the Lord has risen upon me.

Isaiah 65:24

And it shall come to pass, that before they call, I will answer; and while they are yet speaking, I will hear.
(personal confession)

I confess with my mouth, and believe in my heart that it shall come to pass, that before I call, He will answer; and while I am yet speaking, God will hear.

Jeremiah 1:5

Before I formed thee in the belly I knew thee; and before thou camest forth out of the womb I sanctified thee, and I ordained thee a prophet unto the nations.
(personal confession)

I confess with my mouth, and believe in my heart that the Lord knew me before he

formed me in the belly; and before I came forth out of the womb he sanctified me, and ordained me.

Jeremiah 1:12

Then said the Lord unto me, Thou hast well seen: for I will hasten my word to perform it.
(personal confession)

I confess with my mouth, and believe in my heart that I have well seen: for the Lord will hasten His word to perform my desires.

Jeremiah 29:12-13

Then shall ye call upon me, and ye shall go and pray unto me, and ye will hearken unto me. And ye shall seek me, and find me, when ye shall search for me with all your heart.
(personal confession)

I confess with my mouth, and believe in my heart that when I call upon the Lord, and go and pray to him, that he will hear me. I shall seek him, and find him, when I have search for him with all my heart.

Jeremiah 33:3

Call unto me, and I will answer thee, and show thee great and mighty things, which thou knowest not.

(personal confession)

I confess with my mouth, and believe in my heart that when I call to the Lord, that he will answer me, and show me great and mighty things.

Lamentations 3:22-25

It is of the Lord's mercies that we are not consumed, because his compassions fail not, they are new every morning; great is thy faithfulness. The Lord is my portion, saith my soul; therefore will I hope in him. The Lord is good unto them that wait for him, to the soul that seeketh him.

(personal confession)

I confess with my mouth, and believe in my heart that because of the Lord's mercies that I am not consumed, because his compassions fail not, they are new to me every morning; great is his faithfulness. The Lord is my por-

tion, saith my soul; therefore will I hope in him. The Lord is good to me and I do wait for him, and my soul does seek him.

Ezekiel 12:28

There shall none of my words be prolonged any more, but the word which I have spoken shall be done, saith the Lord God.

(personal confession)

I confess with my mouth, and believe in my heart that the Lord's words will not be prolonged any longer in my situation, but the word which He have spoken shall be done, for the Lord is God.

Ezekiel 37:14

And God shall put his spirit in you, and ye shall live, and I shall placed you in your own land: then shall ye know that I the Lord have spoken it, and performed it, saith the Lord.

(personal confession)

I confess with my mouth, and believe in my heart that the Lord has put his spirit in me,

and I shall live, and the Lord have placed me in my own land: I know the Lord have spoken it, and performed it.

Joel 2:28-29

And it shall come to pass afterward, that I will pour out my Spirit upon all flesh; and your sons and your daughters shall prophesy, your old men shall dream dreams, your young men shall see visions: And also upon the servants and upon the handmaids in those days will I pour out my spirit.

(personal confession)

I confess with my mouth, and believe in my heart that it shall come to pass afterward, that the Lord will pour out his Spirit upon all flesh; and my sons and my daughters shall prophesy, our old men shall dream dreams, our young men shall see visions: And also upon the servants and upon the handmaids in my day will He pour out his spirit.

Amos 3:7

Surely the Lord God will do nothing, but he revealeth his secrets unto his servant the prophets.

(personal confession)

I confess with my mouth, and believe in my heart that the Lord God will do nothing, but he reveals his secrets unto me his servant.

Zechariah 4:6

This is the word of the Lord saying, Not by might, nor by power, but by my spirit, saith the Lord of host.
(personal confession)

I confess with my mouth, and believe in my heart that it is Not by might, nor by power, but by my spirit, saith the Lord of host.

Matthew 7:7-8

Ask, and it shall be given you; seek, and ye shall find; knock, and it shall be opened unto you; For every one that asketh receives and he that seeketh findeth; and to him that knocketh it shall be opened.
(personal confession)

I ask, and it is given to me; I seek, and I do find; I knock, and the door is opened to me;

For every one that asketh receiveth; and he that seeketh findeth; and to him that knocketh it shall be opened.

Matthew 13:16-17

But blessed are your eyes, for they see: and your ears, for they hear, for verily I say unto you, that many prophets and righteous men have desired to see those things which ye see, and have not seen them; and to hear those things which ye hear and have not heard them.

(personal confession)

I confess with my mouth, and believe in my heart that many prophets and kings have desired to see those things which I see, and have not seen them; and to hear those things which I hear, and have not heard them.

Matthew 21:22

And all things, whatsoever ye shall ask in prayer, believing, ye shall receive.

(personal confession)

I confess with my mouth, and believe in my heart that all things, whatsoever I shall ask in prayer, believing, I have received.

Mark 9:23

If I canst believe, all things are possible to me who believeth.

Mark 13:31

Heaven and earth shall pass away: but my words shall not pass away.

(personal confession)

I confess with my mouth, and believe in my heart that heaven and earth shall pass away: but my trust in the Lord's words shall not pass away.

Mark 16:15-18

Go ye into all the world, and preach the gospel to every creature. He that believeth and is baptized shall be saved; but he that believeth not shall be damned.

And these signs shall follow them that believe; In my name shall they cast out devils; they shall speak with new tongues; they shall take up serpents; and if they drink any deadly thing, it shall not hurt them; they shall lay hands on the sick, and they shall recover.

(personal confession)

I confess with my mouth, and believe in my heart that, I am going into all the world, and preaching the gospel to every person. He that believes and is baptized shall be saved; but he that believes not shall be damned. And these signs are following me who believe; In Jesus name and through Jesus I am casting out devils; I am speaking with new tongues; I am taking up serpents; and if I drink any deadly thing, it will not hurt me; I am laying hands on the sick, and they are recovering.

Luke 1:45

And blessed is she who believe: for there shall be a performance of those things which were told her from the Lord.

(personal confession)

I confess with my mouth, and believe in my heart that I am blessed because I believe: for there is a performance of those things which were told to me from the Lord.

Luke 4:18

The Spirit of the Lord is upon me, because he hath anointed me to preach the gospel to the poor; he hath sent me to heal the broken-hearted, to preach deliverance to the captives, and recovering of sight to the blind, to set at liberty them that are bruised, to preach the acceptable year of the Lord.

Luke 10:24

For I tell you, that many prophets and kings have desired to see those things which ye see, and have not seen them; and to hear those things which ye hear, and have not heard them.

(personal confession)

I confess with my mouth, and believe in my heart that many prophets and kings have de-

sired to see those things which I see, and have not seen them; and to hear those things which I hear, and have not heard them.

Luke 12:11-12

Take ye no thought how or what thing I shall answer, or what I shall say; for the Holy Ghost shall teach you in the same hour what ye ought to say.

(personal confession)

I confess with my mouth, and believe in my heart that I take no thought how or what thing I shall answer, or what I shall say; for the Holy Ghost shall teach me in the same hour what I ought to say.

St. John 14:12-14

Verily, Verily, I say unto you, He that believeth on me, the works that I do shall you do also; and greater works than these shall you do; because I go unto my Father. And whatsoever ye shall ask in my name, that will I do, that the Father may be glorified in the Son. If ye shall ask anything in my name, I will do it.

(personal confession)

I confess with my mouth, and believe in my heart that, the works that Jesus did shall I do also; and greater works than these shall I do; because he has gone unto the Father. And whatsoever I shall ask in Jesus name, that will he do, that the Father may be glorified in the Son. If I shall ask anything in Jesus Christ name, he will do it.

St. John 14:26

But the Comforter, which is the Holy Ghost, whom the Father will send in my name, he shall teach you all things, and bring all things to your remembrance whatsoever I have said unto you.

(personal confession)

I confess with my mouth, and believe in my heart that the Comforter, who is the Holy Ghost, whom the Father have sent in Jesus name, he shall teach me all things, and bring all things to my remembrance whatsoever the Lord have said to me.

St. John 15:7

If ye abide in me, and my words abide in you, ye shall ask what ye will, and it shall be done unto you.

(personal confession)

I confess with my mouth, and believe in my heart that when I abide in Jesus, and his words abide in me, I shall ask what I want, and it shall be done for me.

St. John 15:16

Ye have not chosen me, but I have chosen you, and ordained you, that ye should go and bring forth fruit, and that your fruit should remain: that whatsoever ye shall ask of the Father in my name, he may give it to you.

(personal confession)

I confess with my mouth, and believe in my heart that Jesus chose and ordained me, and that I am going and bringing forth fruit and my fruit is remaining: and whatsoever I ask of the Father in Jesus name, he will give it to me.

St. John 16:13

Howbeit when he, the Spirit of truth, is come, he will guide you into all truth: for he shall not speak of himself; but whatsoever he shall hear, that shall he speak: and he will shew you things to come.

(personal confession)

I confess with my mouth, and believe in my heart that when he, the Spirit of truth, is come, he does guide me into all truth: for he is not speaking of himself; but whatsoever he hears, that does he speak: he also shows me things to come.

Acts 1:8

But ye shall receive power after that the Holy Ghost is come upon you; and ye shall be witnesses unto me both in Jerusalem, and in all Judaea, and in Samaria, and unto the uttermost part of the earth.

(personal confession)

I confess with my mouth, and believe in my heart that I have receive power after the Holy Ghost has came upon me; and I am a witness unto Jesus both at home, and in all

the city, and in all nations, and unto the uttermost part of the earth.

Acts 2:3-4

And there appeared unto them cloven tongues like as of fire, and it sat upon each of them. And they were filled with the Holy Ghost, and began to speak with other tongues, as the Spirit gave them utterance.
(personal confession)

I confess with my mouth, and believe in my heart that cloven tongues like fire, have come upon me. I am filled with the Holy Ghost, and I speak with other tongues, as the Spirit gives me utterance.

Acts 4:13

Now when they saw the boldness of Peter and John, and perceived that they were unlearned and ignorant men, they marveled; and they took knowledge of them, that they had been with Jesus.

(personal confession)

I confess with my mouth, and believe in my heart that as I dwell with Jesus that boldness and knowledge have been given to me.

Acts 4:31

And when they had prayed, the place was shaken where they were assembled together; and they were all filled with the Holy Ghost, and they spake the word of God with boldness.

(personal confession)

I confess with my mouth, and believe in my heart that as I pray that I will be filled with the Holy Ghost and speak the word of God with boldness.

Acts 18:9-10

Be not afraid, but speak, and hold not they peace: for I am with thee, and no man shall set on thee to hurt thee: for I have much people in this city.

(personal confession)

I confess with my mouth, and believe in my heart that I shall speak, and hold not my peace: for the Lord is with me, and no man shall set on me to hurt me: for the Lord have much people in this city.

Acts 26:16-18

But rise and stand upon thy feet: for I have appeared unto thee for this purpose, to make thee a minister and a witness both of these things which thou hast seen, and of those things in which I will appear unto thee; delivering thee from the people, and from the Gentiles, unto whom now I send thee. To open their eyes, and to turn them from darkness to light, and from the power of Satan unto God, that they may receive forgiveness of sins, and inheritance among them which are sanctified by faith that is in me.

(personal confession)

I confess with my mouth, and believe in my heart that I will rise and stand upon my feet: for the Lord have appeared unto me for this

purpose, to make me a minister and a witness both of these things which the Lord have shown me, and of those things in which the Lord will appear unto me; delivering me from the people, and from the Gentiles, unto whom now he send me.

To open their eyes, and to turn them from darkness to light, and from the power of Satan unto God, that they may receive forgiveness of sins, and inheritance among them which are sanctified by faith that is in God.

Romans 8:31

What shall we then say to these things? If God be for us, who can be against us?
(personal confession)

I confess with my mouth, and believe in my heart that God is for me, no one can be against me?

1 Corinthians 2:9-16

But as it is written, Eye hath not seen, nor ear heard, neither have entered into the heart

of man, the things which God hath prepared for them that love him.

But God hath revealed them unto us by his Spirit: for the Spirit searcheth all things, yea, the deep things of God.

For what man knoweth the things of a man, save the spirit of man which is in him? Even so the things of God knoweth no man, but the Spirit of God.

Now we have received, not the spirit of the world, but the spirit which is of God; that we might know the things that are freely given to us of God.

Which things also we speak, not in the words which man's wisdom teacheth, but which the Holy Ghost teacheth; comparing spiritual things with spiritual.

But the natural man receiveth not the things of the Spirit of God: for they are foolishness unto him: Neither can he know them, because they are spiritually discerned.

But he that is spiritual judgeth all things, yet he himself is judged of no man.

For who hath known the mind of the Lord, that he may instruct him? But we have the mind of Christ.

(personal confession)

I confess with my mouth, and believe in my heart that as it is written, my eyes have not seen, nor my ears heard, but it has entered into my heart, the things which God have prepared for me who love Him.

Because God have revealed them to me by his Spirit: for the Spirit searches all things, yes, the deep things of God.

For what man knows the things of a man, save the spirit of man which is in him? Even so the things of God knows no man, but the Spirit of God.

Now I have received, not the spirit of the world, but the spirit which is of God; that I might know the things that are freely given to me of God.

Which things also I speak, not in the words which man's wisdom teaches, but which the Holy Ghost teaches comparing spiritual things with spiritual.

But the natural man receives not the things of the Spirit of God; for they are foolishness to him: Neither can he know them, because they are spiritually discerned.

But I am spiritual who judge all things, yet I myself is judged of no man. For who have known the mind of the Lord, that he may instruct me? But I have the mind of Christ.

Ephesians 1-17

That the God of our Lord Jesus Christ, the Father of glory may give unto you the spirit of wisdom and revelation in the knowledge of him: The eyes of your understanding being enlightened; that ye may know what is the hope of his calling, and what the riches of the glory of his inheritance in the saints.

(personal confession)

I confess with my mouth, and believe in my heart that God of my Lord Jesus Christ, the Father of glory have given to me the spirit of wisdom and revelation in the knowledge of him: That my eyes are enlightened with understanding.

Ephesians 3:20

Now unto him that is able to do exceeding abundantly above all that we ask or think, according to the power that worketh in us.

(personal confession)

I confess with my mouth, and believe in my heart that God is able to do exceeding abundantly above all that I ask or think, according to the power that works in me.

Ephesians 6:10-19

Finally, my brethren, be strong in the Lord, and in the power of his might.

Put on the whole armour of God, that ye may be able to stand against the wiles of the devil.

For we wrestle not against flesh and blood, but against principalities, against powers, against the rulers of the darkness of this world, against spiritual wickedness in high places.

Wherefore take unto you the whole armor of God, that ye may be able to withstand in the evil day, and having done all to stand,

Stand therefore, having your loins girt about with Truth, and having on the breastplate of righteousness.

And your feet shod with the preparation of the gospel of peace.

Above all, taking the shield of faith, where-with ye shall be able to quench all the fiery darts of the wicked.

And take the helmet of salvation, and the sword of the Spirit, which is the word of God:

Praying always with all prayer and supplication in the Spirit, and watching thereunto with all perseverance and supplication for all saints;

And for me, that Utterance may be given unto me, that I may open my mouth boldly, to make known the mystery of the gospel.
(personal confession)

I confess with my mouth, and believe in my heart that I am strong in the Lord, and in the power of his might.

I do have on the whole armor of God, that I may stand against the wiles of the devil.

For I wrestle not against flesh and blood, but against principalities, against powers, against the rulers of the darkness of this world, against spiritual wickedness in high places.

Wherefore I take unto myself the whole armor of God, that I am able to withstand in the evil day, and having done all to stand,

I do stand therefore, having my loins girt about with truth, and having on the breast plate of righteousness;

And my feet shod with the preparation of the gospel of peace;

Above all, I am able to quench all the fiery darts of the wicked.

And I take the helmet of salvation, and the sword of the Spirit, which is the word of God;

Praying always with all prayer and supplication in the Spirit, and watching thereunto with all perseverance and supplication for all saints;

And for me, that Utterance is given to me, that I may open my mouth boldly, to make known the mystery of the gospel.

Philippians 4:13

I can do all things through Christ which strengtheneth me.

Colossians 1:9-10

Desire that ye might be filled with the knowledge of his will in all wisdom and spiritual understanding. That ye might walk worthy of the Lord unto all pleasing being fruitful in every good work, and increasing in the knowledge of God.

(personal confession)

I confess with my mouth, and believe in my heart that I am filled increasingly with the

knowledge of God's will in all wisdom and spiritual understanding. Being worthy of the Lord and pleasing him, and being fruitful in every good work.

James 1:5

If any of you lack wisdom, let him ask of God, that giveth to all men liberally and upbraideth not; and it shall be given him.

(personal confession)

I confess with my mouth, and believe in my heart that when I ask God for wisdom he gives it to me liberally.

James 3:17

But the wisdom that is from above is first pure, then peaceable, gentle, and easy to be intreated, full of mercy and good fruits, without partiality, and without hypocrisy.

(personal confession)

I confess with my mouth, and believe in my heart that I have received wisdom from God

has manifested in me first pure, then peaceable, gentle, it is easy to be intreated full of mercy and good fruits, without partiality, and without hypocrisy.

1 John 5:14-15

And this is the confidence that we have in him, that, if we ask anything according to his will, he heareth us: and if we know that he hear us, whatsoever we ask, we know that we have the petitions that we desired of him.
(personal confession)

I confess with my mouth, and believe in my heart that I know that the confidence that I have in God, that when I ask anything according to his will, he does hear me: and I know that he hear me, and whatsoever I ask, I know that I have the petitions that I desired of him.

Revelation 2:17

He that hath an ear, let him hear what the Spirit saith unto the churches; To him that overcometh will I give to eat of the hidden manna.

(personal confession)

I confess with my mouth, and believe in my heart that I have an ear to hear what the Spirit says to me. I am an overcomer and therefore, I do eat of the hidden manna of God.

I have an ear to hear the Spirit of God

I have the mind of Christ

I am led by the Holy Spirit

I walk in the wisdom of God

I have insight and foresight

I have the discernment of God

I walk in the knowledge of God

I am instructed by the Holy Ghost

I meditate in the word of God daily

I have understanding of God's word

I have the Revelation Gifts operating in my
life mightily

TO

SPEAK

LIKE

GOD

When God created this world He spoke it into existence.

Genesis 1:3,6,9,11,14,20,24,26

And God said, Let there be light: and there was light. And God saw the light, that it was good; and God divided the light from the darkness.

And God said, Let there be a firmament in the midst of the waters, and let it divide the waters from the waters.

And God Said, Let the waters under the heaven be gathered together unto one place, and let the dry land appear: and it was so.

And God said, Let the earth bring forth grass, the herb yielding seed, and the fruit tree yielding fruit after his kind, whose seed: is in itself, upon the earth and it was so.

And God said, Let there be lights in the firmament of the heaven to divide the day from

seasons, and for days, and years: And let them be for lights in the firmament of the heaven to give light upon the earth: and it was so.

And God said, Let the waters bring forth abundantly the moving creature that hath life, and fowl that may fly above the earth in the open firmament of the heaven.

And God said, Let the earth bring forth the living creature after his kind, cattle, and creeping thing, and beast of the earth after his kind: and it was so.

And God said, Let us make man in our image, after our likeness: and let them have dominion over the fish of the sea, and over the fowl of the air, and over the cattle, and over all the earth, and over every creeping thing that creepeth upon the earth.

So God created man in his own image, in the image of God created he him; male and female created he them.

And God blessed them, and God said unto them, Be fruitful, and multiply, and replenish the earth, and subdue it: and have dominion over the fish of the sea, and over the fowl of the air, and over every living thing that moveth upon the earth.

And God said, Behold, I have given you every herb bearing seed, which is upon the face of all the earth, and every tree, in the which is the fruit of the tree yielding seed; to you it shall be for meat.

And to every beast of the earth, and to every fowl of the air, and to every thing that creepeth upon the earth, wherein there is life, I have given every green herb for meat: and it was so.

Therefore, because we are made in the image and the likeness of God, and we are his heir then we are to also speak things into creation.

At church the praise was high, and prophecy came forth, and the people were edified.

During my quiet time with God, I have praise and worship, and I enjoy speaking in my heavenly tongue. I know the Holy Spirit is in intercession for me, and working out what I need in my life. I am also strengthening my inner man.

At a nursing home with other sisters in Christ, the ladies were praying for the people. I began to sing in tongues, and this lady asked, "Are you from Africa?" Because it sounds like you are singing in African. I answered "No I'm not from Africa." There is a great possibility that I was singing in African. This is what the bible calls divers kinds of tongues.

My sisters in Christ and I were asked to do praise service at this church. I began to sing in tongues, when people suddenly began to cry out, fall to the floor, and praise God. It was as though they were hearing the voice of God. I give God all the Glory.

There have been times when someone have stood up and began to prophesy, and then sat down when they were finished. Someone else would stand up and give the interpretation of what was said.

We must listen carefully to the Holy Spirit to follow his direction. He said that He would instruct us and teach us in the way that we should go, and that He would guide us with his eye. Therefore, have an ear to hear the Spirit of the Lord.

A prayer life is essential to have a relationship with the Holy Spirit. You must take time out of your day to pray.

Ask God to increase your prayer life, and to also give you interpretation of tongues. This is God's wisdom that He is sharing with you. Giving you answers to your questions, and helping you to change to be a better person.

Prophecy

Is speaking supernaturally to men, to say what God says. It is to confirm or foretell future events. It is to edify, comfort and is for exhortation.

(1Cor 12:10) (1Cor 14:3)

Tongues

Is the evidence or the infilling of the Holy Spirit. It is to magnify God by the using of your heavenly tongue. It is to build up yourself spiritually.

(Acts 2:4) (Acts 10:46) (Jude1:20)

Interpretation of Tongues

The supernatural speaking in tongues of a language that one does not understand. To interpret in English what someone else has spoken by the gift of tongues which is to edify the church.

(1Cor 14:4)

67

Numbers 14:28

As truly as I live, saith the Lord, as ye have spoken in mine ears, so will I do to you.

(personal confession)

I confess with my mouth, and believe in my heart that surely as God lives, as I have spoken into his ears, he will do it for me.

Numbers 23:19

God is not a man, that he should lie, neither the son of man, that he should repent: hath he said, and shall he not do it? Or hath he spoken, and shall he not make it good? Behold, I have received commandment to bless: and he hath blessed; and I cannot reverse it.

(personal confession)

I confess with my mouth, and believe in my heart that God is not a man, that he should lie, neither the son of man, that he should repent: he have said, and he have done it? he have spoken, and he have made it good? God have given commandment to bless me: and he is blessing me; and no one can reverse it.

Joshua 1:5

There shall not any man be able to stand before thee all the days of thy life; as I was with Moses, so I will be with thee: I will not fail thee nor forsake thee.

(personal confession)

I confess with my mouth, and believe in my heart that there shall not any man be able to stand before me all the days of my life; as God was with Moses, so He is with me: He will not fail me, nor forsake me.

II Chronicles 16:9

For the eyes of the Lord run to and fro throughout the whole earth, to shew himself strong in the behalf of them whose heart is perfect toward him.

(personal confession)

I confess with my mouth, and believe in my heart that the eyes of the Lord run to and fro throughout the whole earth, to show himself strong in the behalf of me whose heart is perfect toward him.

Job 22:28

Thou shalt also decree a thing, and it shall be established unto thee: and the light shall shine upon thy ways.

(personal confession)

I confess with my mouth, and believe in my heart that when I decree a thing, it is established unto me: and the light does shine upon my ways.

Job 33:14-17

For God speaketh once, yea twice, yet man perceiveth it not. In a dream, in a vision of the night, when deep sleep falleth upon men, in slumberings upon the bed. Then he openeth the ears of men, and sealeth their instruction. That he may withdraw man from his purpose, and hide pride from man.

(personal confession)

I confess with my mouth, and believe in my heart that God speaketh once, yea twice, yet I perceiveth it not. In a dream, in a vision of the night, when deep sleep fall upon me, in slumberings upon my bed; then he open my ears, and seals my instruction. That he may withdraw me from my purpose, and hide

pride from me.

Psalms 20:6

Now know I that the Lord saveth his anointed: he will hear him from his holy heaven with the saving strength of his right hand.

(personal confession)

I confess with my mouth, and believe in my heart that the Lord saves his anointed: he does hear me from his holy heaven with the saving strength of his right hand.

Psalms 21:2

Thou hast given him his heart's desire, and has not withholden the request of his lips.

(personal confession)

I confess with my mouth, and believe in my heart that God have given me my heart's desire, and have not with held the request of my lips.

Psalms 32:8

I will instruct thee and teach thee in the way which thou shalt go: I will guide thee with

mine eye.

(personal confession)

I confess with my mouth, and believe in my heart that the Holy Ghost will instruct me and teach me in the way which I shall go: he will guide me with his eye.

Psalms 34:13

Keep thy tongue from evil and thy lips from speaking guile.

(personal confession)

I confess with my mouth, and believe in my heart that I will keep my tongue from evil, and thy lips from speaking deceitfully.

Psalms 37:5

Commit thy way unto the Lord: trust also in him and he shall bring it to pass.

(personal confession)

I confess with my mouth, and believe in my heart that I will commit my way unto the Lord: I trust also in him and he shall bring my desires to pass.

Psalm 57:2

I will cry unto God most high unto God that performs all things for me.

Psalm 81:10

I am the Lord thy God, which brought thee out of the land of Egypt: open thy mouth wide, and I will fill it.

(personal confession)

I confess with my mouth, and believe in my heart that God have brought me out of my tribulation: and I will open my mouth wide and God will fill it.

Psalm 89:34

My covenant will I not break, nor alter the thing that is gone out of my lips.

(personal confession)

I confess with my mouth, and believe in my heart that God will not break His covenant with me, nor alter the thing that is gone out of His lips.

Psalm 103:5

Who satisfieth thy mouth with good things; so that thy youth is renewed like the eagle's.

(personal confession)

I confess with my mouth, and believe in my heart that God satisfies my mouth with good things; and my youth is renewed like the eagle's.

Proverbs 3:5

Trust in the Lord with all thine heart; and lean not unto thine own understanding. In all thy ways acknowledge him, and he shall direct thy paths.

(personal confession)

I confess with my mouth, and believe in my heart that I trust in the Lord with all my heart; and in all my ways I acknowledge him, and he does direct my paths.

Proverbs 4:20-22

My son, attend to my words; incline thine ear unto my sayings. Let them not depart

from thine eyes; keep them in the midst of thine heart. For they are life unto those that find them, and health to all their flesh.

(personal confession)

I confess with my mouth, and believe in my heart that I attend to the Lords words; I incline my ear unto his sayings. I shall not allow them not to depart from my eyes; and I will keep them in the midst of my heart.

Proverbs 4:24

Put away from thee a froward mouth, and perverse lips put far from thee.

(personal confession)

I confess with my mouth, and believe in my heart that I will put away from myself a froward mouth, and perverse lips.

Proverbs 8:6-8

Hear; for I will speak of excellent things; and the opening of my lips shall be right things. For my mouth shall speak truth; and wickedness is an abomination to my lips. All the words of my mouth are in righteousness; there is nothing froward or perverse in them.

Proverbs 12:14

A man shall be satisfied with good by the fruit of his mouth: and the recompense of a man's hands shall be rendered unto him.

(personal confession)

I confess with my mouth, and believe in my heart that I shall be satisfied with the good fruit of my mouth: and the recompense of my hands shall be rendered unto me.

Proverbs 15:1

A soft answer turneth away wrath: but grievous words stir up anger.

(personal confession)

I confess with my mouth, and believe in my heart that I will turn away wrath with a soft answer, and I will not stir up anger with grievous words.

Proverbs 15:2

The tongue of the wise useth knowledge aright; but the mouth of fools poureth out foolishness.

(personal confession)

I confess with my mouth, and believe in my heart that I use wise knowledge right, and I shall not speak foolishness.

Proverbs 15:4

A wholesome tongue is a tree of life: but perverseness therein is a breach in the spirit.
(personal confession)

I confess with my mouth, and believe in my heart that I have a wholesome tongue which is good for my spirit.

Proverbs 15:7

The lips of the wise disperse knowledge: but the heart of the foolish doeth not so.
(personal confession)

I confess with my mouth, and believe in my heart that I speak wise knowledge.

Proverbs 15:22

Without counsel purposes are disappointed: but in the multitude of counselors they are established.

(personal confession)

I confess with my mouth, and believe in my heart that in a multitude of counselors my answers will be established.

Proverbs 15:23

A man hath joy by the answer of his mouth: and a word spoken in due season, how good it is.

(personal confession)

I confess with my mouth, and believe in my heart that I will answer with joy, and I will speak a word in due season.

Proverbs 15:26

The thoughts of the wicked are an abomination to the Lord: but the words of the pure are pleasant words.

(personal confession)

I confess with my mouth, and believe in my heart that my thoughts, and my words are pleasant to the Lord.

Proverbs 15:28

The heart of the righteous studieth to answer: but the mouth of the wicked poureth out evil things.

(personal confession)

I confess with my mouth, and believe in my heart that my heart is righteous, and I think before I answer.

Proverbs 18:20

A man's belly shall be satisfied with the fruit of his mouth; and with the increase of his lips shall he be filled.

(personal confession)

I confess with my mouth, and believe in my heart that my belly shall be satisfied with the fruit of my mouth; and with the increase of my lips I shall be filled.

Proverbs 18:21

Death and life are in the power of the tongue: and they that love it shall eat the fruit thereof.

(personal confession)

I confess with my mouth, and believe in my heart that death and life are in the power of my tongue: and I shall eat the fruit thereof.

Proverbs 19:5

A false witness shall not be unpunished, and he that speaketh lies shall not escape.

(personal confession)

I confess with my mouth, and believe in my heart that I will not be a false witness.

Proverbs 28:11

A fool uttereth all his mind: but a wise man keepeth it in till afterwards.

(personal confession)

I confess with my mouth, and believe in my heart that I am a wise person who keep my comments to myself.

Proverbs 30:5

Every word of God is pure: he is a shield unto them that put their trust in him.

(personal confession)

I confess with my mouth, and believe in my heart that every word of God is pure: he is a shield unto me and I put my trust in him.

Isaiah 50:4-5

The Lord God have given me the tongue of the learned, that I should know how to speak a word in season to him that is weary: He wakeneth morning by morning, he wakeneth mine ear to hear as the learned. The Lord God have opened mine ear, and I was not re-bellious, neither turned away back.

Isaiah 55:11

So shall my word be that goeth forth out of my mouth; it shall not return unto me void, but it shall accomplish that which I please, and it shall prosper in the thing whereto I sent it.

(personal confession)

I confess with my mouth, and believe in my heart that when God's word goes forth out of his mouth; it does not return unto him void,

but it does accomplish that which he please, and it does prosper in the thing whereto He sent it.

Jeremiah 1:5

Before I formed thee in the belly, I knew thee; and before thou camest forth out of the womb I sanctified thee, and I ordained thee a Prophet unto the nations.

(personal confession)

I confess with my mouth, and believe in my heart that the Lord knew me before he formed me in the belly; and before I came forth out of the womb he sanctified me, and ordained me in my calling.

Jeremiah 15:16

Thy words were found, and I did eat them; and thy word was unto me the joy and rejoicing of mine heart; for I am called by thy name, O Lord God of hosts.

(personal confession)

I confess with my mouth, and believe in my heart that when I eat of the word of the Lord

they are joy and rejoicing to my heart; because I am called by the name of the Lord God of hosts.

Jeremiah 23:21

I have not sent these prophets, yet they ran: I have not spoken to them, yet they prophesied.

(personal confession)

I confess with my mouth, and believe in my heart that if God did not call me to be a prophet I will not run as a prophet, and if he have not spoken to me, I will not prophesy.

Jeremiah 23:28

The prophet that hath a dream, let him tell a dream; and he that hath my word, let him speak my word faithfully.

(personal confession)

I confess with my mouth, and believe in my heart that if I have a dream I shall tell my dream, but if I have a word from the Lord I will speak His word faithfully.

Jeremiah 23:31

Behold, I am against the prophets, saith the Lord, that use their tongues, and say, He saith. Behold, I am against them that prophesy also dreams, saith the Lord, and do tell them and cause my people to err by their lies, and by their lightness: yet I sent them not.
(personal confession)

I confess with my mouth, and believe in my heart that I do not prophesy lies or dreams, therefore, the Lord is not against me.

Jeremiah 27:18

But if they be prophets, and if the word of the Lord be with them, let them now make intercession to the Lord of hosts.
(personal confession)

I confess with my mouth, and believe in my heart that I am called to be a prophet, and I have the word of the Lord in my mouth, therefore will I make intercession to the Lord.

Jeremiah 33:3

Call unto me, and I will answer thee, and show thee great and mighty things, which thou knowest not.

(personal confession)

I confess with my mouth, and believe in my heart that when I call the Lord, He will answer me, and show me great and mighty things.

Lamentations 3:22-25

It is of the Lord's mercies that we are not consumed, because his compassions fail not, they are new every morning; great is thy faithfulness. The Lord is my portion, saith my soul; therefore will I hope in him. The Lord is good unto them that wait for him, to the soul that seeketh him.

(personal confession)

I confess with my mouth, and believe in my heart that because of the Lord's mercies that I am not consumed, because his compassions fail not, they are new to me every morning; great is thy faithfulness. The Lord is my portion, says my soul; therefore will I hope in

him. The Lord is good unto me who wait for him, to the soul that seek him.

Zechariah 8:16

These are the things that ye shall do; Speak ye every man the truth to his neighbour; excute the judgment of truth and peace in your Gates.

(personal confession)

I confess with my mouth, and believe in my heart that I shall speak to every man the truth and also to my neighbor; I shall excute judgment of truth and peace in my boarders.

Matthew 7:15

Beware of false prophets, which come to you in sheep's clothing, but inwardly they are ravening wolves.

(personal confession)

I confess with my mouth, and believe in my heart that I shall be aware of false prophets.

Matthew 10:19

When they deliver you up, take no thought how or what ye shall speak: for it shall be given you in that same hour what ye shall speak.

(personal confession)

I confess with my mouth, and believe in my heart that I shall take no thought how or what I shall speak; for it shall be given to me in the same hour by the Holy Ghost what I shall speak.

Matthew 17:20-21

For verily I say unto you. If ye have faith as a grain of mustard seed, ye shall say unto this mountain. Remove hence to yonder place; and it shall remove; and nothing shall be impossible unto you. Howbeit this kind goeth not out but by prayer and fasting.

(personal confession)

I confess with my mouth, and believe in my heart that I have great faith, and I shall say to my situation, move and it shall move, and nothing shall be impossible to me.

However some spirits go not out but by prayer and fasting.

Mark 16:15-18

Go ye into all the world, and preach the gospel to every creature. He that believeth and is baptized shall be saved; but he that believeth not shall be damned. And these signs shall follow them that believe; In my name shall they cast out devils; they shall speak with new tongues;. they shall take up serpents; and if they drink any deadly thing, it shall not hurt them; they shall lay hands on the sick, and they shall recover.

(personal confession)

I confess with my mouth, and believe in my heart that, I am going into all the world, and preaching the gospel to every person. He that believes and is baptized shall be saved; but he that believes not shall be damned. And these signs are following me who believe; In Jesus name I am casting out devils; I am speaking with new tongues;. I am taking up serpents; and if I drink any deadly thing, it shall not hurt me; I am laying hands on the sick,

and they are recovering.

Luke 4:18

The Spirit of the Lord is upon me, because he hath anointed me to preach the gospel to the poor; he hath sent me to heal the broken-hearted, to preach deliverance to the captives, and recovering of sight to the blind, to set at liberty them that are bruised, To preach the acceptable year of the Lord.

Luke 11:9-10

And I say unto you, Ask, and it shall be given you; Seek, and ye shall find; Knock, and it shall be opened unto you. For every one that asketh receiveth; and he that seeketh findeth; and to him that knocketh it shall be opened.

(personal confession)

I confess with my mouth, and believe in my heart that when I ask, it is given to me; and when I seek, I do find; and when I knock, the door is opened to me. For every one that ask receives; and he that seek do find; and to him that knock the door is opened.

Luke 12:11-12

Take ye no thought how or what thing ye shall answer, or what ye shall say; For the Holy Ghost shall teach you in the same hour what ye ought to say.

(personal confession)

I confess with my mouth, and believe in my heart that I take no thought how or what thing I shall answer, or what I shall say; for the Holy Ghost shall teach me in the same hour what I ought to say.

St. John 8:12

I am the light of the world: he that followeth me shall not walk in darkness, but shall have the light of life.

(personal confession)

I confess with my mouth, and believe in my heart that Jesus is the light of the world: I do follow him and I do not walk in darkness, but I do have the light of life.

St. John 14:12-14

Verily, Verily, I say unto you, He that believeth on me, the works that I do shall you do also; and greater works than these shall you do; because I go unto my Father and whatsoever ye shall ask in my name, that will I do, that the Father may be glorified in the Son. If ye shall ask anything in my name, I will do it.

(personal confession)

I confess with my mouth, and believe in my heart that, the works that Jesus did shall I do also; and greater works than these shall I do; because he has gone unto the Father. And whatsoever I shall ask in Jesus name, that will he do, that the Father may be glorified in the Son. If I shall ask anything in Jesus name, he will do it.

St. John 14:26

But the Comforter, which is the Holy Ghost, whom the Father will send in my name, he shall teach you all things, and bring all things to your remembrance whatsoever I have said unto you.

(personal confession)

I confess with my mouth, and believe in my heart that Holy Ghost will teach me all things and bring all things to my remembrance.

St. John 15:7

If ye abide in me, and my words abide in you, ye shall ask what ye will, and it shall be done unto you.

(personal confession)

I confess with my mouth, and believe in my heart that when I abide in Jesus, and his words abide in me, I shall ask what I want, and it shall be done for me.

St. John 15:16

Ye have not chosen me, but I have chosen you, and ordained you, that ye should go and bring forth fruit, and that your fruit should remain: that whatsoever ye shall ask of the Father in my name, he may give it to you.

I confess with my mouth, and believe in my heart that I have been chosen by Jesus and ordained. I am going and bringing forth fruit and my fruit is remaining: and whatsoever I shall ask of the Father in Jesus name, he will give it to me.

St. John 16:13

Howbeit when he, the Spirit of truth, is come, he will guide you into all truth: for he shall not speak of himself; but whatsoever he shall hear, that shall he speak: and he will shew you things to come.

(personal confession)

I confess with my mouth, and believe in my heart that when he, the Spirit of truth, is come, he is guiding me into all truth: for he is not speaking of himself; but whatsoever he hears, that does he speak: and he does show me things to come.

Acts 18:9-10

Be not afraid, but speak, and hold not thy peace: for I am with thee, and no man shall set on thee to hurt thee: for I have much people in this city.

(personal confession)

I confess with my mouth, and believe in my heart that I am not afraid, but I shall speak, and hold not my peace: for the Lord is with me, and no man shall set on me to hurt me: for the Lord have much people in this city.

Acts 26:16-18

But rise and stand upon thy feet: for I have appeared unto thee for this purpose, to make thee a minister and a witness both of these things which thou hast seen, and of those things in which I will appear unto thee; delivering thee from the people, and from the Gentiles, unto whom now I send thee, to open their eyes, and to turn them from darkness to light, and from the power of Satan unto God, that they may receive forgiveness of sins, and inheritance among them which are sanctified by faith that is in me.

(personal confession)

I confess with my mouth, and believe in my heart that I will rise and stand upon my feet: for the Lord have appeared unto me for this purpose, making me a minister and a witness both of these things which the Lord have shown me, and of those things in which the Lord will appear unto me; delivering me from the people, and from the Gentiles, unto whom now he send me. To open their eyes, and to turn them from darkness to light, and from the power of Satan unto God, that they may receive forgiveness of sins, and inheritance among them which are sanctified by faith that is in Jesus.

Romans 12:6

Having then gifts differing according to the grace that is given to us whether prophecy, let us prophesy according to the proportion of faith.

(personal confession)

I confess with my mouth, and believe in my heart that I will prophesy according to my faith.

1 Corinthians 14:1-2

Follow after charity, desire spiritual gifts, but rather ye may prophesy. For he that speaketh in an unknown tongue speaketh not unto men, but unto God: for no man understandeth him; howbeit in the spirit he speaketh mysteries.

(personal confession)

I confess with my mouth, and believe in my heart that I do love my neighbor, and I desire spiritual gifts and prophecy. When I speak in tongues I am speaking to God who is giving me mysteries.

1 Corinthians 14:3-4

He that prophesieth speaketh unto men to edification, and exhortation, and comfort. He that speaketh in an unknown tongue edifieth himself; but he that prophesieth edifieth the church.

(personal confession)

I confess with my mouth, and believe in my heart that when I prophesy unto men I prophesy edification, exhortation and comfort unto the church. But when I speak in an unknown tongue I edify myself.

1 Corinthians 14:13

Wherefore, let him that speaketh in an unknown tongue pray that he may interpret.
(personal confession)

I confess with my mouth, and believe in my heart that when I speak in tongues I ask for the interpretation that the mysteries of God are revealed to me.

1 Corinthians 14:14

For if I pray in an unknown tongue, my spirit prayeth, but my understanding is unfruitful. What is it then? I will pray with the spirit, and I will pray with the understanding also: I will sing with the spirit, and I will sing with the understanding also.
(personal confession)

I confess with my mouth, and believe in my heart that I am praying in the spirit, and I am praying with the understanding: I am singing in the spirit, and I am singing with the understanding.

1 Corinthians 14:27-28

If any man speak in an unknown tongue, let it be by two or at the most three, and that by course, and let one interpret. But if there be no interpreter let him keep silent in the church: and let him speak to himself and to God.

(personal confession)

I confess with my mouth, and believe in my heart that if I speak in an unknown tongue, and it be by two or three, let one interpret. But if there be no interpreter I will keep silent in the church, and speak to God.

1 Corinthians 14:32-33

The spirit of the prophets are subject to the prophets. For God is not the author of confusion, but of peace, as in all churches of the saints.

(personal confession)

I confess with my mouth, and believe in my heart that when I prophesy in tongues I am in control, For God is not the author of confusion, but of peace, as in all churches of the saints.

1 Corinthians 14:39-40

Wherefore, brethren, covet to prophesy, and forbid not to speak with tongues. Let all thing be done decently and in order.

(personal confession)

I confess with my mouth, and believe in my heart that I desire to prophesy, and to speak with tongues. I allow all thing to be done decently and in order.

1 Corinthians 15:33

Be not deceived: evil communications corrupt good manners.

(personal confession)

I confess with my mouth, and believe in my heart that I am not deceived: evil communications corrupt good manners.

Ephesians 4:29

Let no corrupt communication proceed out of your mouth, but that which is good to the use of edifying, that it may minister grace unto the hearers.

(personal confession)

I confess with my mouth, and believe in my heart that I will let no corrupt communication proceed out of my mouth, but that which is good to the use of edifying, that it may minister grace unto the hearers.

Hebrew 13:5-6

Let your conversation be without covetousness; and be content with such things as ye have: for he hath said, I will never leave thee nor forsake thee. So that we may boldly say, The Lord is my helper, and I will not fear what man shall do unto me.

(personal confession)

I confess with my mouth, and believe in my heart that my conversation is without covetousness; and I am content with such things as I have: for the Lord have said, He will never leave me, nor forsake me. So that I may boldly say, The Lord is my helper and I will not fear what man shall do unto me.

Hebrew 13:15-16

By him therefore let us offer the sacrifice of praise to God continually, that is the fruit of our lips giving thanks to his name. But to do good and to communicate forget not: for with such sacrifices God is well pleased.

(personal confession)

I confess with my mouth, and believe in my heart that I shall offer the sacrifice of praise to God continually, that the fruit of my lips will give thanks to his name. I shall do good and to communicate and forget not: for wich such sacrifices God is well pleased.

James 1:5

If any of you lack wisdom, let him ask of God, that giveth to all men liberally and up-braideth not; and it shall be given him.

(personal confession)

I confess with my mouth, and believe in my heart that if I lack wisdom I shall ask of God that giveth to all men liberally and upbraideth no; and it shall be given to me.

James 1:19

Wherefore, my beloved brethren, let every man be swift to hear, slow to speak, slow to Wrath.

(personal confession)

I confess with my mouth, and believe in my heart that I will be swift to hear, slow to speak, and slow to wrath.

James 5:16

Confess your faults one to another, and pray one for another, that ye may be healed. The effectual fervent prayer of a righteous man availeth much.

(personal confession)

I confess with my mouth, and believe in my heart that I will confess my faults to a trusted one, and pray for another that they may be healed. The effectual fervent prayer of a righteous man avails much.

James 5:20

Let him know, that he which converteth the sinner from the error of his way, shall save a soul from death, and shall hide a multitude of sins.

(personal confession)

I confess with my mouth, and believe in my heart that I shall convert the sinner from the error of his way, and shall save a soul from death, and shall hide a multitude of sins.

1 Peter 1:15

But as he which hath called you is holy, so be ye holy in all manner of conversation.

(personal confession)

I confess with my mouth, and believe in my heart that God is holy, so shall I be holy in all manner of my conversation.

1 Peter 3:10

For he that will love life, and see good days, let him refrain his tongue from evil, and his lips that they speak no guile.

(personal confession)

I confess with my mouth, and believe in my heart that I love life, and I see good days, I will refrain my tongue from evil, and my lips that they speak no deceit.

1 Peter 3:15

Sanctify the Lord God in your hearts: and be ready always to give an answer to every man that asketh you a reason of the hope that is in you with meekness and fear.

(personal confession)

I confess with my mouth, and believe in my heart that I shall sanctify the Lord God in my heart: and I shall be ready to give an answer to every man that ask me for a reason of the hope that I have in Jesus Christ with respect.

2 Peter 1:21

For prophecy came not in old time by the will of man; but by Holy men of God speak as they were moved by the Holy Ghost.

(personal confession)

I confess with my mouth, and believe in my heart that I do not prophesy of my own will, but as I am moved by the Holy Ghost.

Revelation 2:17

He that hath an ear, let him hear what the Spirit saith unto the churches. To him that overcometh will I give to eat of the hidden manna.

(personal confession)

I confess with my mouth, and believe in my heart that I have an ear to hear what the Spirit says unto me. I am an overcomer and therefore, I do eat of the hidden manna of God.

I have an ear to hear the Spirit of God

I have a quiet spirit

I speak in tongues daily

I am led by the Holy Spirit

I know prophecy is in my mouth

I am instructed by the Holy Ghost

I open my mouth and the Lord fills it

I ask for the interpretation of tongues
and God gives it to me

I am here to encourage, edify and comfort

I operate in the gifts that God have given
to me

I have the Utterance Gifts operating in
my life mightily

TO

DO

LIKE

GOD

While watching different deliverance ministries on television I am in amazement of all the different healings that take place. I have been diagnose with Fibromaylgia which is a (chronic pain disorder). I have had prayer, and I believe that God is going to heal me. I know the time will come when I walk into my healing.

On the other hand, I wish I could have been one of those people that suffered with the same illness. They received a miracle! They were healed instantly after receiving prayer.

I can't say that I haven't experienced the Gift of Faith. It was at a time when my husband and I needed to change our residence. I was in prayer, and the Lord told me that I had a house by water.

He revealed to me (1) we were going to see the house on a Sunday (2) we were going to put down a certain amount of money to hold the house, and (3) we knew the person who would connect us with the real estate broker.

Everything happened just the way the Lord said, but before the manifestation of it, several obstacles were in our way.

Being unmoved in our faith we now live by the Little Calumet River, and we are enjoying it everyday.

Why haven't you use the Gift of Faith for this illness Sister Jefferson? <u>I Believe God!</u> and that is enough faith.

God have given some of us the ministry of healing and deliverance, and we are to believe his word.

He is our Heavenly Father and we are to do like him. We have that part of Him in our spirit as an heir of God.

JOMP

Healing

The gifts of healing has different manifestations of healing taking place. To supernaturally heal all manner of sickness and diseases.
(Matt 4:23-24) (Matt 10:1) (Ps 107:20)

Miracles

The working of miracles is a supernatural act that man cannot deny.
(Exodus 14:16) (Matt 14:19-20)
(John 11:41-43) (Acts 4:16)

Faith

The gift of faith is to receive the manifestation of a thing that seem to be impossible.
(Gen 17:16) (Dan 3:16) (Matt 8:10)
(Mark 10:52) (Rom 4:17-20)

Exodus 15:26

If thou wilt diligently hearken to the voice of the Lord thy God, and wilt do that which is right in his sight, and wilt give ear to his commandments, and keep all his statutes, I will put none of these diseases upon thee which I have brought upon the enemy; for I am the Lord that healeth thee.

(personal confession)

I confess with my mouth, and believe in my heart that because I am diligently listening to the voice of the Lord my God, and I am doing what is right in his sight, and I am l giving ear to his commandments, and I am keeping all of his statues, He will not put any diseases upon me which he have brought upon my enemy; for he is the Lord that heals me.

Joshua 1:5

There shall not any man be able to stand before thee all the days of my life; as God was with Moses, so I will be with thee: I will not fail thee, nor forsake thee.

(personal confession)

I confess with my mouth, and believe in my heart that there shall not any man be able to stand before me all the days of my life; as God was with Moses, so He is with me: He will not fail me, nor forsake me.

II Chronicles 7:14

If my people, which are called by my name, shall humble themselves, and pray, and seek my face, and turn from their wicked ways, then will I hear from heaven, and will forgive their sin, and will heal their land.

(personal confession)

I confess with my mouth, and believe in my heart that I am called by Jesus name and therefore I shall humble myself and pray, and seek God's face, I have turned from my wicked ways, and God have heard from heaven and have forgiven my sin, and have healed my land.

II Chronicles 16:9

For the eyes of the Lord run to and fro throughout the whole earth, to shew himself

strong in the behalf of them whose heart is perfect toward him.

(personal confession)

I confess with my mouth, and believe in my heart that the eyes of the Lord run to and fro throughout the whole earth, to show himself strong in the behalf of me whose heart is perfect toward him.

Job 6:8

Oh that I might have my request; and that God would grant me the thing that I long for!

(personal confession)

I confess with my mouth, and believe in my heart that I have received my request; and that God has granted me the things that I have longed for.

Job 22:21

Acquaint now thyself with him, and be at peace, thereby good shall come unto thee.

(personal confession)

I confess with my mouth, and believe in my heart that I have acquainted myself with the Lord, and I am at peace, good also has come to me.

Psalm 20:6

Now know I that the Lord saveth his anointed; he will hear him from his holy heaven with the saving strength of his right hand.

(personal confession)

I confess with my mouth, and believe in my heart that the Lord saveth his anointed: he will hear me from his holy heaven with the saving strength of his right hand.

Psalm 30:2

O Lord my God, I cried unto thee, and thou has healed me.

Psalm 34:7-8

The angel of the Lord encampeth round about them that fear him, and delivereth

them. O taste and see that the Lord is good: blessed is the man that trusteth in him.

(personal confession)

I confess with my mouth, and believe in my heart that the angel of the Lord is encamped around about me, and He have delivered me. The Lord is good to me.

Psalm 34:17-22

The righteous cry, and the Lord heareth, and delivereth them out of all their troubles. The Lord is nigh unto them that are of a broken heart; and saveth such as be of a contrite spirit. Many are the afflictions of the righteous; but the Lord delivereth him out of them all.

(personal confession)

I confess with my mouth, and believe in my heart that I am the righteous of God and when I cry unto him, the Lord hear and delivered me out of all my troubles. The Lord is near them that are of a broken heart; and save such as be of a contrite spirit.

Psalm 41:2-3

The Lord will preserve him, and keep him alive; and he shall be blessed upon the earth: and thou wilt not deliver him unto the will of his enemies. The Lord will strengthen him upon the bed of languishing: thou wilt make all his bed in his sickness.

(personal confession)

I confess with my mouth, and believe in my heart that the Lord will preserve me, and keep me alive; and I shall be blessed upon the earth: and he will not deliver me unto the will of my enemy. The Lord will strengthen me upon the bed of my languishing: he will restore my health.

Psalm 57:2

I will cry unto God most high: unto God that performeth all things for me.

Psalm 84:11

For the Lord is a sun and shield: The Lord will give grace and glory; no good thing will he withhold from them that walk uprightly.

116

(personal confession)

I confess with my mouth, and believe in my heart that the Lord is a sun and shield: The Lord will give grace and glory; no good thing will he withhold from me who walk uprightly.

Psalm 90:17

And let the beauty of the Lord our God be upon us: and establish thou the work of our hands upon us; yea, the work of our hands establish thou it.

(personal confession)

I confess with my mouth, and believe in my heart that the beauty of the Lord my God is upon me: and has established the work of my hands; yes, the work of my hands are established by the Lord.

Psalm 103:1-2

Bless the Lord, O my soul, and forget not all his benefits: who forgiveth all thine iniquities; who healeth all thy diseases.

(personal confession)

I confess with my mouth, and believe in my heart that I do bless the Lord with all my soul, and I have not forgotten all of His benefits: who have forgiven all of my iniquities; and have healed all of my diseases.

Psalm 107:20

He sent his word, and healed them, and delivered them from their destructions.

(personal confession)

I confess with my mouth, and believe in my heart that when the Lord sent his word, he healed me, and delivered me from all my destructions.

Proverbs 16:24

Pleasant words are as an honeycomb, sweet to the soul, and health to the bones.

(personal confession)

I confess with my mouth, and believe in my heart that my words are as an honeycomb, sweet to my soul, and health to my bones.

Isaiah 41:10

Fear thou not; for I am with thee: be not dismayed; for I am thy God: I will strengthen thee; yea, I will help thee; yea, I will uphold thee with the right hand of my righteousness.

(personal confession)

I confess with my mouth, and believe in my heart that I do not fear; for the Lord is with me: I am not dismayed; because he is my God: he is strengthening me; yes, he is helping me; yes, he is upholding me with the right hand of his righteousness.

Isaiah 53:5

But he was wounded for our transgressions, he was bruised for our iniquities: the chastisement of our peace was upon him; and with his stripes we are healed.

(personal confession)

I confess with my mouth, and believe in my heart that Jesus was wounded for my transgressions, he was bruised for my iniquities: the chastisement of my peace was upon him; and with his stripes I am healed.

Isaiah 54:17

No weapon that is formed against thee shall prosper; and every tongue that shall rise against thee in judgment thou shalt condemn. This is the heritage of the servants of the Lord, and their righteousness is of me, saith the Lord.

(personal confession)

I confess with my mouth, and believe in my heart that no weapon that is formed against me or my family shall prosper; and every tongue that shall rise against us in judgment thou shall condemn. This is the heritage of the servants of the Lord, and their righteousness is of me, said the Lord.

Isaiah 60:1

Arise, shine; for thy light is come, and the glory of the Lord is risen upon thee.

(personal confession)

I confess with my mouth, and believe in my heart that I shall arise and shine; for thy light is come, and the glory of the Lord is risen upon me.

Isaiah 61:1

The spirit of the Lord God is upon me; because the Lord hath anointed me to preach good tidings unto the meek; he hath sent me to bind up the broken hearted, to proclaim liberty to the captives, and the opening of the prison to them that are bound; to proclaim the acceptable year of the Lord, and the day of vengeance of our God; to comfort all that mourn.

Jeremiah 17:14

Heal me, O Lord and I shall be healed; save me, and I shall be saved: for thou art my praise.

Jeremiah 30:17

I will restore health unto thee, and I will heal thee of thy wounds, saith the Lord.

(personal confession)

I confess with my mouth, and believe in my heart that the Lord have restored health to me and have healed me of my wounds, the Lord have spoken it.

Lamentations 3:25

The Lord is good unto them that wait for him, to the soul that seeketh him.

(personal confession)

I confess with my mouth, and believe in my heart that the Lord is good to me and I do wait for him, my soul also seek him.

Matthew 4:23

And Jesus went about all Galilee, teaching in their synagogues; and preaching the gospel of the kingdom, and healing all manner of sickness and all manner of disease among the people.

(personal confession)

I confess with my mouth, and believe in my heart that I will do as Jesus, teaching in the churches and preaching of the kingdom and healing all manner of disease among the people.

Matthew 4:24

And his fame went throughout all Syria and they brought unto him all sick people that

were with divers diseases and torments, and those which were possessed with devils, and those which were lunatic, and those that had the palsy; and he healed them.

(personal confession)

I confess with my mouth, and believe in my heart that I will do as Jesus did. People will bring to me all sick people with different diseases and torments, and those which are possessed with devils, and those which are lunatic, and those that have the palsy; and they shall be healed in Jesus name.

Matthew 8:16

When the even was come they brought unto him many that were possessed with devils: and he cast out the spirits with His word, and healed all that were sick.

(personal confession)

I confess with my mouth, and believe in my heart that I will do as Jesus did. They will bring unto me many that are possessed with devils: and I will cast out the spirits with the Word of Jesus, and all that are sick shall be healed.

Matthew 10:1

He gave them power against unclean spirits, to cast them out, and to heal all manner of sickness and all manner of disease.

(personal confession)

I confess with my mouth, and believe in my heart that Jesus gave me power against unclean spirits, to cast them out, and to heal all manner of sickness and all manner of disease.

Matthew 17:20-21

For verily I say unto you. If ye have faith as a grain of mustard seed, ye shall say unto this mountain. Remove hence to yonder place; and it shall remove; and nothing shall be impossible unto you. Howbeit this kind goeth not out but by prayer and fasting.

(personal confession)

I confess with my mouth, and believe in my heart that I do have faith as a grain of mustard seed, I shall say unto this illness remove hence to yonder place; and it shall be remove; and nothing shall be impossible unto me. Howbeit some sickness goes not out but by prayer and fasting.

Matthew 21:22

And all things, whatsoever ye shall ask in prayer, believing ye shall receive.

(personal confession)

I confess with my mouth, and believe in my heart that all things whatsoever I shall ask in prayer, believing I shall receive.

Mark 9:23-29

If thou canst believe, all things are possible to him that believeth. This kind can come forth by nothing, but by prayer and fasting.

(personal confession)

I confess with my mouth, and believe in my heart that I do believe that all things are possible to me. I know that some spirits can come forth by nothing, but by prayer and fasting.

Mark 10:52

Go thy way; thy faith hath made thee whole.

(personal confession)

I confess with my mouth, and believe in my heart that my faith have made me whole.

Mark 16:15-18

Go ye into all the world and preach the gospel to every creature. He that believeth and is baptized shall be saved; but he that believeth not shall be damned. And these signs shall follow them that believe; In my name shall they cast out devils; they shall speak with new tongues; they shall take up serpents; and if they drink any deadly thing, it shall not hurt them; they shall lay hands on the sick and they shall recover.

(personal confession)

I confess with my mouth, and believe in my heart that I am going into all the world and preaching the gospel to every person. He that believes and is baptized shall be saved; but he that believes not shall be damned. And these signs are following me who believe; In Jesus name I am casting out devils; I am speaking with new tongues; I am taking up serpents; and if I drink any deadly thing, it shall not hurt me; I am laying hands on the sick and they are recovering.

Luke 1:45

And blessed is she who believe: for there shall be a performance of those things which were told to them from the Lord.

(personal confession)

I confess with my mouth, and believe in my heart that I am blessed and I do believe: for there shall be a performance of those things which were told to me from the Lord.

Luke 4:18

The Spirit of the Lord is upon me, because he hath anointed me to preach the gospel to the poor; he hath sent me to heal the broken-hearted, to preach deliverance to the captives, and recovering of sight to the blind, to set at liberty them that are bruised, to preach the acceptable year of the Lord.

Luke 10:19

Behold, I give unto you power to tread on serpents and scorpions, and over all the power of the enemy: and nothing shall by any means hurt you.

(personal confession)

I confess with my mouth, and believe in my heart that Jesus gave to me power to tread on serpents and scorpions, and over all the power of the enemy: and nothing shall by any means hurt me.

Luke 11:9-10

And I say unto you, Ask, and it shall be given you; Seek, and ye shall find; Knock, and it shall be opened unto you. For every one that asketh receiveth; and he that seeketh findeth; and to him that knocketh it shall be opened.

(personal confession)

I confess with my mouth, and believe in my heart that when I ask, it is given to me; and when I seek, I do find; and when I knock, the door is opened to me. For every one that ask receives; and he that seeks finds; and to him that knock it shall be opened.

St. John 8:12

I am the light of the world: he that followeth me shall not walk in darkness, but shall have the light of life.

(personal confession)

I confess with my mouth, and believe in my heart that Jesus is the light of the world: I do follow him and I do not walk in darkness, but I do have the light of life.

St. John 14:12-14

Verily, Verily, I say unto you, He that believeth on me, the works that I do shall you do also; and greater works than these shall you do; because I go unto my Father. And whatsoever ye shall ask in my name, that will I do, that the Father may be glorified in the Son. If ye shall ask anything in my Name, I will do it.

(personal confession)

I confess with my mouth, and believe in my heart that, the works that Jesus did shall I do also; and greater works than these shall I do; because he has gone unto the Father. And whatsoever I shall ask in Jesus name, that will he do, that the Father may be glorified in the Son. If I shall ask anything in Jesus name, he will do it.

St. John 15:16

Ye have not chosen me, but I have chosen you, and ordained you, that ye should go and bring forth fruit, and that your fruit should remain: that whatsoever ye shall ask of the Father in my name, he may give it to you.

(personal confession)

I confess with my mouth, and believe in my heart that I have been chosen by Jesus and ordained. I am going to bring forth fruit, and my fruit shall remain, and whatsoever I shall ask of the Father in Jesus name, he shall given it to me.

Acts 1:8

But ye shall receive power after that the Holy Ghost is come upon you; and ye shall be witnesses unto me both in Jerusalem and in all Judaea, and in Samaria, and unto the uttermost part of the earth.

(personal confession)

I confess with my mouth, and believe in my heart that I have received power after the Holy Ghost came upon me; I am a witnesses to God both at home and in all the city, and

to nations, and unto the uttermost part of the earth.

Romans 1:17

For therein is the righteousness of God revealed from faith to faith: as it is written, the just shall live by faith.

(personal confession)

I confess with my mouth, and believe in my heart that I am the righteousness of God, and that I do live from faith to faith: as it is written, the just shall live by faith.

Romans 8:31

What shall we then say to these things? If God be for us, who can be against us?

(personal confession)

I confess with my mouth, and believe in my heart that God is for me, so who can be against me?

Romans 8:37

Nay, in all these things we are more than conquerors through him that loved us. For I am persuaded, that neither death, nor life, nor angels, nor principalities, nor powers, nor things present, nor things to come, nor height, nor depth, nor any other creature, shall be able to separate us from the love of God, which is in Christ Jesus our Lord.

(personal confession)

I confess with my mouth, and believe in my heart that in all these things I am more than a conqueror through him that loved me. For I am persuaded, that neither death, nor life, nor angels, nor principalities, nor powers, nor things present, nor things to come, nor height, nor depth, nor any shall keep me from the love of God, which is in Christ Jesus my Lord.

Ephesians 3:20

Now unto him that is able to do exceeding abundantly above all that we ask or think, according to the power that worketh in us.

(personal confession)

I confess with my mouth, and believe in my heart that God is able to do exceeding abundantly above all that I ask or think, according to the power that works in me.

Ephesians 6:10-19

Finally, my brethren, be strong in the Lord, and in the power of his might.

Put on the whole armor of God, that ye may be able to stand against the wiles of the devil.

For we wrestle not against flesh and blood, but against principalities, against powers, against the rulers of the darkness of this world, against spiritual wickedness in high places.

Wherefore take unto you the whole armor of God, that ye may be able to withstand in the evil day, and having done all to stand.

Stand therefore, having your loins girt about with Truth, and having on the breastplate of righteousness;

And your feet shod with the preparation of the gospel of peace;

Above all, taking the shield of faith, where-with ye shall be able to quench all the fiery darts of the wicked.

And take the helmet of salvation, and the sword of the Spirit, which is the word of God:

Praying always with all prayer and supplication in the Spirit, and watching thereunto with all perseverance and supplication for all saints;

And for me, that Utterance may be given unto me, that I may open my mouth boldly, to make known the mystery of the gospel.

(personal confession)

I confess with my mouth, and believe in my heart that I am strong in the Lord, and in the power of his might.

I do have on the whole armor of God, that I may stand against the wiles of the devil.

For I wrestle not against flesh and blood, but against principalities, against powers, against the rulers of the darkness of this world, against spiritual wickedness in high places.

Wherefore I take unto myself the whole armor of God, that I am able to withstand in the evil day, and having done all to stand.

I do stand therefore, having my loins girt about with truth, and having on the breastplate of righteousness;

And my feet shod with the preparation of the gospel of peace;

Above all, I take the shield of faith, wherewith I shall be able to quench all the fiery darts of the wicked.

And I take the helmet of salvation, and the sword of the Spirit, which is the word of God:

Praying always with all prayer and supplication in the Spirit, and watching thereunto with all perseverance and supplication for all saints;

And for me, utterance have been given to me, and I boldly make known the mystery of the gospel.

Philippians 4:13

I can do all things through Christ which strengtheneth me.

James 1:5

If any of you lack wisdom, let him ask of God, that giveth to all men liberally and upbraideth not; and it shall be given him.

(personal confession)

I confess with my mouth, and believe in my heart that when I ask God that he give wisdom to me liberally.

1 John 5:14-15

And this is the confidence that we have in him, that, if we ask anything according to his will, he heareth us: And if we know that he hear us, whatsoever we ask, we know that we have the petitions that we desired of him.

(personal confession)

I confess with my mouth, and believe in my heart that I know the confidence that I have in God, that if I ask anything according to his will, he hears me: and if I know that he hear me, whatsoever I ask, I know that I have the petitions that I desired of him.

3 John 2

Beloved, I wish above all things that thou mayest prosper and be in health, even as thy soul prospereth.

(personal confession)

I confess with my mouth, and believe in my heart that I am prospering, and I am in great health, because my soul is prospering.

Revelation 2:17

He that hath an ear, let him hear what the Spirit saith unto the churches. To him that overcometh will I give to eat of the hidden manna.

(personal confession)

I confess with my mouth, and believe in my heart that I have an ear to hear what the Spirit says to me. I am an overcomer therefore, will God give me to eat of the hidden manna.

I have an ear to hear the Spirit of God

I have healing hands

I am one of God generals

I am called to heal the sick

I am anointed for miracles

I have the power of healing in me

I am instructed by the Holy Ghost

I am doing the works that Jesus did

I have the gift of faith working in me

I lay hands on the sick and they recover

I have the Power Gifts operating in my
life mightily

WEALTH
CONFESSIONS!

Not by Might,

Nor by Power,

But by my Spirit,

Saith the Lord
of Host.

Zechariah 4:6

God being our Father, and we being his heirs we are to do like our Father. God spoke us into existences and created us in his image and after his likeness.

Therefore, we are creators, and we are to speak into existence the things that we want to be, have, and do into our lives.

We are to speak those things which are not as though they were. We can speak God's word regarding our finances.

Listen to the Holy Spirit and He will give you an answer how to get out of debt. He will reveal to you a talent, a gift, an invention that will bring you out of debt.

Speak the word of God everyday, and see yourself out of debt. Meditation is one of the most powerful practices that you can have, because vision is what you see. If you can see it, and believe it you can have it. Psalms 118:25 –Save now, I beseech thee, O Lord: O Lord, I beseech thee, send now prosperity.

Deuteronomy 8:1

All the commandments which I command thee this day shall ye observe to do, that ye may live, and multiply, and go in and possess the land which the Lord sware unto your fathers.

(personal confession)

I confess with my mouth, and believe in my heart that I am observing to do all that the Lord commands me this day, and He is multiplying me.

Deuteronomy 8:18

But thou shall remember the Lord thy God: for it is he that giveth thee power to get wealth.

(personal confession)

I confess with my mouth, and believe in my heart that I remember the Lord my God: for it is he that giveth me power to get wealth.

Deuteronomy 12:20

The Lord thy God shall enlarge thy border, as he hath promised thee.

(personal confession)

I confess with my mouth, and believe in my heart that the Lord my God have enlarged my border, as he have promised me.

Deuteronomy 15:6

For the Lord thy God blesseth thee, as he promised thee: and thou shalt lend unto many nations, but thou shalt not borrow.

(personal confession)

I confess with my mouth, and believe in my heart that the Lord my God have blessed me, as he promised, I shall lend and not borrow.

Deuteronomy 16:15

God shall bless thee in all thine increase, and in all the works of thine hands, therefore thou shalt surely rejoice.

(personal confession)

I confess with my mouth, and believe in my heart that God has bless me in all mine increase, and in all the works of my hands, therefore I will surely rejoice.

Deuteronomy 28:2

And all these blessings shall come on thee, and overtake thee, if thou shalt hearken unto the voice of the Lord thy God. Bless shalt thou be in the city, and blessed shalt thou be in the field.

(personal confession)

I confess with my mouth, and believe in my heart that all these blessings have come upon me, and have overtake me, because I have listened to the voice of the Lord my God. Therefore, I am bless in the city, and blessed in the field.

Deuteronomy 30:19

I have set before you life and death, blessings and cursing; therefore choose life, that both you and thy seed may live.

(personal confession)

I confess with my mouth, and believe in my heart that God have set before me blessings and cursing; therefore I choose life, that both myself and my seed may live.

Joshua 1:8

This book of the law shall not depart out of thy mouth; but thou shalt meditate therein day and night, that thou mayest observe to do according to all that is written therein: for then thou shalt make thy way prosperous, and then thou shalt have good success.

(personal confession)

I confess with my mouth, and believe in my heart that the book of the law has not departed out of my mouth; but I do meditate in it day and night, that I may observe to do according to all that is written. For the Lord have made my way prosperous, and I do have good success.

1 Chronicles 4:10

And Ja'-bez called on the God of Israel saying, Oh that thou wouldest bless me indeed, and enlarge my coast, and that thine hand might be with me, and that thou wouldest keep me from evil. God granted him that which he requested.

(personal confession)

I confess with my mouth, and believe in my heart that God have blessed me indeed and have enlarge my territory, and his hand is with me, he have kept me from evil and have granted me that which I have requested.

11 Chronicles 15:7

Be ye strong therefore, and let not your hands be weak: for your work shall be rewarded.

(personal confession)

I confess with my mouth, and believe in my heart that the work of my hands are rewarded.

11 Chronicles 26 :5

And he sought God in the days of Zechariah, who had understanding in the visions of God: and as long as he sought the Lord, God made him to prosper.

(personal confession)

I confess with my mouth, and believe in my heart that I have understanding in the vision

of God, and as long as I seek the Lord, God shall make me to prosper.

Nehemiah 2:20

The God of heaven, he will prosper us; therefore we his servants will arise and build.

(personal confession)

I confess with my mouth, and believe in my heart that the God of heaven, he is prospering me; I am being promoted and I am building.

Job 22:21

Acquaint now thyself with him, and be at peace, thereby good shall come unto thee.

(personal confession)

I confess with my mouth, and believe in my heart that I have acquainted myself with God, and I am at peace: thereby good has come to me.

Psalms 1:3

He shall be like a tree planted by the rivers of water that bringeth forth his fruit in his season; his leaf also shall not wither; and whatsoever he doeth shall prosper.

(personal confession)

I confess with my mouth, and believe in my heart that I am like a tree planted by the rivers of water that bringeth forth his fruit in his season; my leaf also shall not wither or fade; and whatsoever I do I shall prosper.

Psalms 18:16-19

He sent from above, he took me, he drew me out of many waters. He delivered me from my strong enemy, and from them which hated me: for they were too strong for me. They prevented me in the day of my calamity: but the Lord was my stay. He brought me forth also into a large place; he delivered me, because he delighted in me.

Psalms 18:25

With the merciful thou will shew thyself merciful: with an upright man thou wilt shew thyself upright.

(personal confession)

I confess with my mouth, and believe in my heart that the Lord will be merciful toward me.

Psalms 33:18:19

Behold, the eye of the Lord is upon them that fear him, upon them that hope in his mercy; to deliver their soul from death, and to keep them alive in famine.

(personal confession)

I confess with my mouth, and believe in my heart that the Lord eye is upon me, his mercy has delivered my soul from death, and has kept me alive in famine.

Psalms 35:27

Let them shout for joy, and be glad, that favour my righteous cause: yea, let them say continually, Let the Lord be magnified, which hath pleasure in the prosperity of his servant.

(personal confession)

I confess with my mouth, and believe in my heart that God takes pleasure in the prosperity of his servant, therefore shall I shout for joy and be glad.

Psalms 37:3

Trust in the Lord, and do good: so shalt thou dwell in the land, and verily thou shalt be fed.

(personal confession)

I confess with my mouth, and believe in my heart that I will trust in the Lord and do good, and I shall dwell in the land of plenty and I shall be fed.

Psalms 37:19

They shall not be ashamed in the evil time: and in the days of famine they shall be satisfied.

(personal confession)

I confess with my mouth, and believe in my heart that I will not be ashamed in the evil day, and in the days of famine I shall be satisfied.

Psalms 37:25

I have been young, and now am old: yet have I not seen the righteous forsaken, nor his seed begging bread.

(personal confession)

I confess with my mouth, and believe in my heart that I have not seen the righteous forsaken, nor my seed begging bread.

Psalms 68:19

Blessed be the Lord, who daily loadeth us with benefits, even the God of our salvation.
(personal confession)

I confess with my mouth, and believe in my heart that the Lord daily load me with benefits.

Psalms 92:13-14

Those that be planted in the house of the Lord shall flourish in the courts of our God. They shall still bring forth fruit in old age: they shall be fat and flourishing.
(personal confession)

I confess with my mouth, and believe in my heart that I am flourishing and bringing forth fruit.

Psalms 103:1-2

Bless the Lord, o my soul: and all that is within me, bless his holy name. Bless the Lord, o my soul and forget not all his benefits.

(personal confession)

I confess with my mouth, and believe in my heart that I will not forget all of the benefits of the Lord.

Psalms 116:14

I will pay my vows unto the Lord now in the presence of all his people.

Psalms 118:5

I called upon the Lord in distress: the Lord answered me, and set me in a large place.

(personal confession)

I confess with my mouth, and believe in my heart that the Lord have set me in a large place.

Proverbs 3:3-4

Let not mercy and truth forsake thee: bind them about thy neck: write them upon the table of thine heart: So shalt thou find favour and good understanding in the sight of God and man.

(personal confession)

I confess with my mouth, and believe in my heart that I have not let mercy and truth forsake me, and I have found favor and good understanding in the sight of God and man.

Proverbs 3:9-10

Honor the Lord with thy substance, and with the firstfruits of all thine increase. So shall thy barns be filled with plenty, and thy presses shall burst out with new wine.

(personal confession)

I confess with my mouth, and believe in my heart that I shall honor the Lord with my capital and sufficiency from my righteous labor, and with the firstfruit of all my income. So shall my bank account be filled with plenty of money, and overflowing.

Proverbs 18:20

A man's belly shall be satisfied with the fruit of his mouth; and with the increase of his lips shall he be filled.

(personal confession)

I confess with my mouth, and believe in my heart that my belly shall be satisfied with the fruit of my mouth; and with the increase of my lips I shall be filled.

Proverbs 28:20

A faithful man shall abound with blessings: but he that maketh haste to be rich shall not be innocent.

(personal confession)

I confess with my mouth, and believe in my heart that, because I am a faithful person I am abounding with blessings.

Proverbs 28:27

He that giveth unto the poor shall not lack: but he that hideth his eyes shall have many a curse.

(personal confession)

I confess with my mouth, and believe in my heart that I do give to the poor and I do not lack anything in my life.

Isaiah 1:19

If ye be willing and obedient, ye shall eat the good of the land.

(personal confession)

I confess with my mouth, and believe in my heart that I am willing and obedient, and I am eating the good of the land.

Isaiah 48:17

Thus saith the Lord, thy redeemer, the Holy One of Israel; I am the Lord thy God which teacheth thee to profit, which leadeth thee by the way that thou shouldest go.

(personal confession)

I confess with my mouth, and believe in my heart that the Lord, my redeemer, the Holy One of Israel; Is the Lord my God who

teaches me how to profit, and He leads me in the way that I should go.

Isaiah 54:2-3

Enlarge the place of thy tent and let them stretch forth the curtains of thine habitations: spare not, lengthen thy cords, and strengthen thy stakes; For thou shalt break forth on the right hand and on the left.

(personal confession)

I confess with my mouth, and believe in my heart that God has enlarged my place and have stretched forth my territory, I am enlarged on the right hand and on the left.

Isaiah 55:11

So shall my word be, that goeth forth out of my mouth: it shall not return unto me void, but it shall accomplish that which I please, and it shall prosper in the thing whereto I sent it.

(personal confession)

I confess with my mouth, and believe in my heart that God's word shall not return unto

him void, but it shall accomplish that which He please, and prosper in the thing where He send it.

Malachi 3:10

Bring ye all the tithes into the storehouse, that there may be meat in mine house, and prove me now herewith saith the Lord of hosts. If I will not open you the windows of heaven, and pour you out a blessing, that there shall not be room enough to receive it.

(personal confession)

I confess with my mouth, and believe in my heart that I am bringing all my tithes into the storehouse, that there may be meat in the Lord's house. The Lord has opened the windows of heaven, and is pouring out blessings for me, that there is not enough room to receive it.

Matthew 7:11

If ye then, being evil, know how to give good gifts unto your children, how much more shall your Father which is in heaven give good things to them that ask him?

(personal confession)

I confess with my mouth, and believe in my heart that my Father which is in heaven give to me good things because I ask him.

Luke 6:38

Give and it shall be given unto you; good measure, pressed down, and shaken together, and running over, shall men give into your bosom. For with the same measure that ye mete withal it shall be measured to you again.

(personal confession)

I confess with my mouth, and believe in my heart that men are giving to me pressed down, and shaken together, and running over.

Acts 20:35

I have shewed you all things, how that so laboring ye ought to support the weak, and to remember the words of the Lord Jesus, how he said, "It is more blessed, to give than to receive."

(personal confession)

I confess with my mouth, and believe in my heart that the Lord have showed me all things, and because I support the weak I am blessed.

Romans 8:32

He that spared not his own Son, but delivered him up for us all, how shall he not with him also freely give us all things.

(personal confession)

I confess with my mouth, and believe in my heart that God shall freely give me all things.

Romans 10:17

So then faith cometh by hearing, and hearing by the word of God.

(personal confession)

I confess with my mouth, and believe in my heart that my faith comes by hearing, and continued hearing of the word of God.

11 Corinthians 1:20

For all of the promises of God in him are yea, and in him A-men; unto the glory of God by us.

(personal confession)

I confess with my mouth, and believe in my heart that all of the promises of God are yes to me.

11 Corinthians 9:6

But this I say, He which soweth sparingly shall reap also sparingly; and he which soweth bountifully shall reap also bountifully.

(personal confession)

I confess with my mouth, and believe in my heart that I do not sow in a small amount, but I sow bountifully therefore I do reap bountifully.

Galatians 3:14

That the blessing of Abraham might come on the Gentiles through Jesus Christ: that we might receive the promise of the Spirit through faith.

(personal confession)

I confess with my mouth, and believe in my heart that I have received the blessings of Abraham through Jesus Christ.

Galatians 6:9

And let us not be weary in well doing: for in due season we shall reap, if we faint not.

(personal confession)

I confess with my mouth, and believe in my heart that I am not weary in well doing: for I am reaping in my due season.

Ephesians 3:20

Now unto him that is able to do exceeding abundantly above all that we ask or think, according to the power that worketh in us.

(personal confession)

I confess with my mouth, and believe in my heart that God is able to do exceeding abundantly above all that I ask or think, according to the power that work in me.

1 Timothy 6:17

Charge them that are rich in this world, that they be not high minded, nor trust in uncertain riches, but in the living God, who giveth us richly all things to enjoy.

(personal confession)

I confess with my mouth, and believe in my heart that I am rich. I will not trust in my riches or be high minded, but I am trusting in the living God who gives me all thing to enjoy.

Hebrews 6:14

Surely blessing I will bless thee, and multiplying I will multiply thee.

(personal confession)

I confess with my mouth, and believe in my heart that God is blessings me, and multiplying me everyday.

3 John 2

Beloved, I wish above all things that thou mayest prosper and be in health, even as thy soul prospereth.

(personal confession)

I confess with my mouth, and believe in my heart that I am prospering, and I am in great health, and my soul is also prospering.

I am a tithe and offering pay master

I will pay my Vow

I walk in success

I have God's favor

I am a multi-millionaire

I have divine connections

I am above and not beneath

I am the head, not the tail.

I am a lender not a borrower

I have prosperity in my hands

I am instructed by the Holy Ghost

I am out of debt and my needs are met

FORGIVENESS

We all have experienced betrayal from someone. A family member, a close friend, or someone who you could not believe wanted to see you hurt.

When the person that we looked up to, a husband, wife, teacher, employer, or pastor does the unforgiveable we think to ourselves I might forgive, but I won't forget.

Disappointments seem to never fade away quickly, but if you have Jesus the disappointment will not only leave you soon, but forgiveness will also be possible.

If you hold onto un-forgiveness you are not hurting that person you really are hurting yourself. Some people hold grudges for years, and the person that they are angry with have forgotten about the matter. They have moved on with their lives and are happy.

Bitterness destroys not only your heart, but your health. More people are ill due to un-forgiveness. They just can't seem to forgive

the person for what they have done.

Maybe you were betrayed by a family member or friend, and even though he/she is now deceased you still hold un-forgiveness in your heart towards them.

I am not saying that what they did was all right, but you must forgive him/her, and move on, because they can not hurt you anymore.

I have heard people say, I came to the church because I thought the people would be so nice to me. I was hurt when I realized that was not true. I don't care where they live, what title they hold, whether they are rich or poor, people are just people.

The scripture says in <u>Psalms 55:12-14</u>: For it was not an enemy that reproached me; then I could have borne it: neither was it he that hated me that did magnify himself against me; then I would have hid myself from him.

But it was thou, a man mine equal, my guide, and mine acquaintance. We took sweet counsel together, and waled unto the house of God in company.

In conclusion, it is important to the Lord that you forgive. He made a new commandment "This is my commandment, that ye love one another, as I have loved you." Don't lose your soul because of un-forgiveness.

FORGIVENESS

To pardon, or show clemency, mercy absolution, or blame.

The act of pardoning somebody for a mistake or wrongdoing. The tendency to forgive offenses readily and easily.

An act that bestows or shows mercy toward another person.

The easing of distress or pain to the one that was hurt. To free somebody from what they did.

Forgiveness for sins, especially in a Christian church.

A spoken blessing used in a Christian church to grant absolution to somebody.

Responsibility for something wrong or unfortunate that has happened.

Exodus 14:13

And Moses said unto the people, Fear ye not, stand still, and see the salvation of the Lord which he will shew to you to day: for the Egyptians whom ye have seen to day, ye shall see them no more for ever.

(personal confession)

I confess with my mouth, and believe in my heart that I will fear not, I will stand still, and see the salvation of the Lord which he will show to me today: for my enemies that I have today, I shall see them no more forever.

Proverbs 14:12

There is a way which seemeth right unto a man, but the end thereof are the ways of death.

(personal confession)

I confess with my mouth, and believe in my heart that man's ways might seem right to him, but the ways of the Lord I do follow.

Proverbs 16:7

When a man's ways please the Lord he maketh even his enemies to be at peace with him.

(personal confession)

I confess with my mouth, and believe in my heart that my ways please the Lord, and he has made my enemies to be at peace with me.

Proverbs 25:21

If thine enemy be hungry give him bread to eat: and if he be thirsty, give him water to drink.

(personal confession)

I confess with my mouth, and believe in my heart that if my enemy be hungry I will give him bread to eat: and if he be thirsty I will give him water to drink.

Matthew 5:44

But I say unto you, love your enemies, bless them that curse you, do good to them, that hate you and pray for them which despitefully use you and persecute you.

(personal confession)

I confess with my mouth, and believe in my heart that I will love my enemies, and bless them that curse me, do good to them that hate me, and pray for them which despitefully use me and persecute me.

Matthew 6:14-15

For if ye forgive men their trespasses, your heavenly Father will also forgive you. But if ye forgive not men their trespasses, neither will your Father forgive you your trespasses.

(personal confession)

I confess with my mouth, and believe in my heart that if I forgive men of their trespasses, my heavenly Father will also forgive me. But if I do not forgive men of their trespasses, neither will my Father forgive me of my trespasses.

Matthew 9:6

But that ye may know that the Son of man hath power on earth to forgive sin.

(personal confession)

I confess with my mouth, and believe in my heart that the Son of man (Jesus) hath power on earth to forgive me of my sins.

Matthew 5:23-24

Therefore, if thou bring thy gift to the altar and there rememberest that thy brother hath aught against thee; leave there thy gift before the altar, and go thy way; first be reconciled to thy brother, and then come and offer thy gift.

(personal confession)

I confess with my mouth, and believe in my heart that if I bring my gift to the altar and there remember that my brother/sister is angry with me, that I will leave my gift at the altar, and first be reconciled to my brother/sister, and then come and offer my gift.

Mark 11:25

And when ye stand praying, forgive if ye have ought against any, that your Father also which is in heaven may forgive you your trespasses. But if ye do not forgive, neither will

your Father which is in heaven forgive your trespasses.

(personal confession)

I confess with my mouth, and believe in my heart that when I stand praying, I will forgive if I have ought against any, that my Father also which is in heaven may forgive my trespasses. But if I do not forgive, neither will my Father which is in heaven forgive my trespasses.

Luke 6:37

Judge not, and ye shall not be judged: condemn not and ye shall not be condemn: forgive, and ye shall be forgiven.

(personal confession)

I confess with my mouth, and believe in my heart that if I Judge not, I shall not be judged: if I condemn not I shall not be condemn: and if I forgive, I shall be forgiven.

Luke 6:41-42

And why beholdest thou the mote that is in thy brother's eye, but perceives not the beam that is in thine own eye? Thou hypocrite. Cast out first the beam out of thine own eye,

and then shalt thou see clearly to pull out the mote that is in thy brother's eye.

(personal confession)

I confess with my mouth, and believe in my heart that I will cast out first the beam that is in my own eye, and then when I see clearly I will pull out the mote that is in my brother's eye.

Romans 12:19

Dearly beloved, avenge not yourselves, but rather give place unto wrath: for it is written vengeance is mine: I will repay saith the Lord.

(personal confession)

I confess with my mouth, and believe in my heart that I will not avenge myself. For it is written vengeance is mine: I will repay saith the Lord.

Ephesians 4:31

Let all bitterness, and wrath and anger, and clamour, and evil speaking, be put away from you with all malice.

(personal confession)

I confess with my mouth, and believe in my heart that I will let all bitterness, and wrath and anger, and clamour, and evil speaking, be put away from me.

Ephesians 4:32

And be ye kind one to another, tenderhearted. Forgiving one another, even as God for Christ's sake hath forgive you.

(personal confession)

I confess with my mouth, and believe in my heart that I will be kind and tenderhearted. Forgiving even as God for Christ's sake have forgiven me.

Philippians 4:8

Finally, brethren, whatsoever things are true, whatsoever things are honest, whatsoever things are just, whatsoever things are pure, whatsoever things are lovely, whatsoever things are of good report: if there be any virtue, and if there be any praise, think on these things.

(personal confession)

I confess with my mouth, and believe in my heart that whatsoever things are true, whatsoever things are honest, whatsoever things are just, whatsoever things are pure, whatsoever things are lovely, whatsoever things are of good report: if there be any virtue, and if there be any praise, I will think on these things.

1 John 1:9

If we confess our sins, he is faithful and just to forgive us our sins, and to cleanse us from all unrighteousness.

(personal confession)

I confess with my mouth, and believe in my heart that If I confess my sins, he is faithful and just to forgive me of my sins, and to cleanse me from all unrighteousness.

STEPS

TO

SALVATION

I WANT TO: KNOW LIKE GOD, SPEAK LIKE GOD & DO LIKE GOD

Now, be That Anointed

Man/Woman

That God Has Called

You to be!

Oh! But First You Must

be on Jesus Christ Team

So, do What it Says on

The Following Poem,

& it Will Show You

How to be Reborn

I Know of No Other

I Know of No Other Who Can
Forgive Your Sins,
And Give You Comfort & Peace Within

There is no Other Who Can
Change Your Life,
And Take Away Hurt, Lying & Strife

Prosperity, Love & Joy Will be a Part of You,
But First There is Something That
You Must do

(One)

Admit That You Are a Sinner,
And You Are on Your Way to
Becoming a Winner

(Two)

Repent & be Godly Sorry For What
You Have Done,
And You Will Have The Chance to Meet
Jesus Christ The Son

(Three)

Confess Your Sins For He Is Faithful
& Just to Forgive,
And Jesus Will Show You A New Way to Live

(Four)

Forsake All Desire For Sin,
And Allow The Lord Jesus Christ
to Come in

(Five)

Believe & Rely on The Son of God,
And Give Him Your Mind, Soul, Strength
& Your Heart

(Six)

Accept That God Is & That He Rose Jesus
From The Grave,
And This my Friend is The Way to be
Forgiven & Saved

Prayer of Salvation

Lord, I come before you acknowledging and admitting that I am a sinner, I repent Lord for the life I have led. I confess and own up to the wrong I have done, but now Lord I want to forsake this life and believe on Jesus, and accept you into my life as my Lord and savior. Lord you said in:

Romans 10:9-10

"That if thou (I) shall confess with thy (my) mouth the Lord Jesus and shall believe in thine (my) heart that God hath raised him from the dead, thou (I) shall be saved. For with the heart man believeth unto righteousness; and with the mouth confession is made unto salvation."

Now Lord Jesus, I pray for my brother/sister who has just given himself/herself to you. Those who are experiencing chronic pain or another type of handicap I ask for their healing. Lord, I know that you are able to do exceeding abundantly above all that we ask or think, according to the power that worketh in us. Ephesians 3:20

Therefore, I am requesting on their behalf to perform a miracle in their body and personal challenges. I know that with men this is impossible; but with God all things are possible with you. <u>Matthew 19:26</u>

Your word tells us to: Ask and shall be given you; Seek and ye shall find; Knock, and it shall be opened unto you;

For every one that asketh receiveth; and he that seeketh findeth; and to him that knocketh it shall be opened. <u>Matthew 7:78</u>

I am asking you to do a great work in them through their deliverance and healing that they might be great witnesses for you.

Help them through the Holy Ghost to seek you with all of their heart that they might find you and know you as their Lord and savior.

Lord, when you knock upon the door of their heart I pray that the door shall be opened, and that they will not harden their heart towards you. That they might dine with you and receive all that you have for them as their Father.

Now Lord, I give you praise for the manifestation of this prayer which have gone up in love. I thank you for receiving them as heirs of God, adopted into the household of faith and made as the righteousness of God in Jesus name.

Amen

Jefferson Outreach Ministries & Publications
Jesus Operates Miracles Profoundly
JOMP Order Form
Chicago, IL 60628 - (773) 928-0712
E-mail - jomplb@sbcglobal.net
Barbara J's Books of Deliverance

Additional Reading Publications

Jesus Poetic Series

All Right Women God Is
Speaking To You!
(J) $15.00

Jesus Is Our Victory!
(E) $15.00

You Are Christ's Anointed Conqueror!
(S) $15.00

Jesus & Relationships
(U) $15.00

You Are God's Chosen Vessel!
(S) $15.00

Additional Reading Publications

Let Me Give You What The
Lord Gave Me,
Down To Earth Poetry
$15.00

I Want To
Know Like God,
Speak Like God
& Do Like God
$15.00

Your Pain Is Not In Vain!
$15.00

Send $15.00 plus $2.50 for Shipping and
Handling PERSONAL CHECKS/ CREDIT
CARDS /MONEY ORDERS ACCEPTED
Allow two to three weeks for your order to be
filled

Thank You For Patronizing
Jefferson Outreach Ministries & Publications
Jesus Operate Miracles Profoundly
JOMP

6-1-09